WINNIPEG'S
GENERAL
STRIKE

WINNIPEG'S GENERAL STRIKE

REPORTS FROM THE FRONT LINES

MICHAEL DUPUIS

Charleston — London

THE
History
PRESS

Published by The History Press
Charleston, SC 29403
www.historypress.net

Copyright © 2014 by Michael Dupuis
All rights reserved

First published 2014

Manufactured in the United States

ISBN 978.1.62619.339.0

Library of Congress CIP data applied for.

CONTENTS

FOREWORD

How refreshing to be reminded that bloggers did not invent conspiracy theories. Nor were they the first to harbour a mistrust of the mainstream media. Bloggers did not invent paranoia, although it often seems that way. That was alive and well in the midst of the 1919 Winnipeg General Strike. It is interesting to ponder how the strike's outcome might have been different had those who opposed it not convinced themselves the strike was a plot by Bolshevists to bring Russian-style revolution to Canada.

"Oh the Reds, the Reds, Reds in our streets," anti-strike media cried. Surely the fear that was whipped up went a long way to prodding the government to call out the troops to charge the strikers and their supporters in their final gathering, the silent parade down Main Street. Certainly, fear was the driving force behind the assault on protesters at that silent parade that earned that day the name "Bloody Saturday."

Did the powers-that-be really believe in the Red threat? Or were their efforts merely to turn the public against the strike? It is amazing how people can behave when their livelihood is threatened. And the strike did threaten the order of things. Life in the mansions on Winnipeg's genteel Wellington Crescent was worlds away from the horrific living conditions in the city's North End. That was what the strike was really about—a living wage, not a revolution.

It's easy to see that now. We have the benefit of knowing the outcome of the provincial inquiry held in the weeks after the strike. Judge H.A. Robson found that the strike was a reaction to low wages and high cost of living. And we know that historian Donald Masters's 1949 investigation determined there was no Bolshevik backing to the strike, a fact seldom disputed by other historians.

Knowing these two facts makes it easy to judge which of the newspaper reports had it right: the strikers' paper or those opposed to the strike. The strike was about what the strikers and their newspapers said it was: the right for labour to organize. That renders this book's structure so interesting.

Michael Dupuis has interspersed reports from the strikers' newspapers with reports from those opposed. Sometimes that creates amusing moments. The strikers' papers urged workers to do nothing, to win by simply doing nothing, while the "anti" papers cited the Citizens Committee of One Thousand urging that something must be done.

Some reports clearly tell both sides of the story. One reporter takes the reader on a walk through the Labor Temple, where the Strike Committee gathers, and then through the headquarters of the Citizens Committee of One Thousand. The writer contrasts the opposing sides' clothes—strikers doff their overalls in favour of their Sunday best, and on anti-strikers: "the Sunday suit of the striker has given way to the tailor's best."

Too few Canadians know the story of the Winnipeg General Strike; even fewer understand its significance. *Winnipeg's General Strike: Reports from the Front Lines* offers a view of what the residents of Winnipeg, of Canada and of the world read about the strike day by day. It's a history lesson from which we can all benefit.

JULIE CARL
Deputy Editor
Winnipeg Free Press

PREFACE

The idea for this book developed from my 1973 MA thesis "The Response of the *Toronto Daily Press* to the Winnipeg General Strike." In late 1972, I interviewed septuagenarian Graham Spry and octogenarian Charles Plewman, both of whom had experienced the strike firsthand. There are some events so intense they are never forgotten, and this was certainly the case for Spry and Plewman with respect to the 1919 strike. Fifty-three years later, they retained vivid memories of the event. Spry had been acquainted with not only several of the dispute's labour leaders but also many of Winnipeg's newspapermen, especially John Dafoe, the longtime editor of the *Manitoba Free Press*. As well, during the strike Spry had been a six-dollar-a-day special constable. Between 1917 and 1921, Charles Plewman was boys secretary of the Winnipeg YMCA. He was also the younger brother of *Toronto Daily Star* reporter William Plewman, who was sent to cover the strike.

As I approached the end of a teaching career in 2004, I returned to my interest in the strike. I spoke with ninety-two-year-old George Plewman, nephew of William Plewman. Then I contacted strike historian Jack Bumsted, who encouraged me to write about the event's press coverage, a subject he acknowledged needed exploration. Given Professor Bumsted's support, in 2005 I wrote an article for *Manitoba History* on the strike's reportorial and editorial coverage by the *Toronto Daily Star*. Soon after, I met Robert and Murray Conklin, the grandsons of John James Conklin, who in 1919 was a veteran newspaperman with the *Manitoba Free Press* and during the strike a freelance writer (stringer) for several Canadian daily papers.

While undertaking further strike research in Winnipeg during 2006, I met CBC producer Andy Blicq, who was preparing *Bloody Saturday*, a television documentary on the strike that later aired in June 2007. Andy took me on a tour of 1919 strike locales, including the CPR train station (now a First Nation's Centre), Vulcan Iron Works, Hell's Alley, the *Winnipeg Telegram* building, the Manitoba legislature and the Ukrainian Labor Temple. In 2010, I began collaborating with Winnipeg producer Danny Schur on his documentary concerning the contradictory evidence surrounding the shooting death of immigrant Mike Sokolowski during the strike's June 21 riot. Schur's *Mike's Bloody Saturday* premiered in Winnipeg in October 2011. Finally, in 2013, I was approached by The History Press to write a book on the strike from the viewpoint of the journalists who experienced and wrote about the event.

In *Communities of Journalism*, David Nord observed that "Historians look back for origins; journalists look ahead for outcomes." As *Winnipeg's General Strike: Reports from the Front Lines* combines elements of history *and* journalism, it is my hope that the book interests professors of history and journalism, students of each discipline, journalists, members of the labour movement, strike aficionados and the general public.

A final note: the press material presented in this book contains "–or" spellings as used in American newspapers for such words as *labour*, *endeavour*, *ardour* and *honour*. At the time of the Winnipeg General Strike, the "–or" spellings were long-established practice in many Canadian newspapers. All press matter in *Winnipeg's General Strike: Reports from the Front Lines* has been reproduced as initially published, with "[*sic*]" following words that were originally misspelled or grammatically incorrect.

ACKNOWLEDGEMENTS

The author is grateful to those who have provided time, resources and courtesies in the development of this publication.

Monica Ball, Reference Services, Manitoba Legislative Library
Gary Becker, Winnipeg Memorabilia Collectors Club
Julie Carl, deputy editor, *Winnipeg Free Press*
Christopher Coutlee, Toronto Reference Library
Chantal Ellingwood, artist
Sharon Foley, archives technician, Archives of Manitoba
Stuart Hay, Manitoba Legislative Library
Lucie Lariviere, library assistant, Greater Victoria Public Library
Library and Archives Canada staff
Katie Orlando, commissioning editor, The History Press
Marie Reidke, archives assistant, Archives of Manitoba
Kate Rutherford, library assistant, Greater Victoria Public Library
Danny Schur, Winnipeg composer/lyricist/writer/producer

INTRODUCTION

Journalism is the first rough draft of history
—Washington Post *publisher Philip Graham*

It is important to remember that with the exception of silent movie newsreels, mass communication in North America in 1919 was primarily print-based. Given that newspapers and magazines were the major print sources, they maintained a dominant and persuasive power to inform and shape public opinion. This was especially true of coverage of major events.

It was also standard practice for editorial writers to take strong positions concerning newsworthy events. As for reporters, freelance writers and magazine and press association correspondents, it was expected that they would provide balanced, objective and fact-based reporting. However, though theoretically impartial, they were not completely detached from the assignment they were covering because of their predetermined personal views and choice of sources. Finally, regardless of experience, very few were able to recall and re-create with 100 percent accuracy details of events that occurred hours or even days earlier.

Before examining the journalists' dispatches and editors' commentaries presented in this book, it will be helpful to understand the historical context of the strike. In November 1917, Russian Marxist Vladimir Lenin successfully led an organization of professional revolutionaries known as Bolsheviks to overthrow the czar, Nicholas II. Following the revolution, a bloody civil war ensued for millions in Russia, and the doctrine of Bolshevism spread to Europe and North America, where it foreshadowed profound societal change. As a result, for nearly three years a nationwide, anti-Communist hysteria known as the "Red Scare" persisted in North America.

During this time, there was widespread alarm, often fanned by the press, over supporters of the Russian Revolution and soviets (workers' councils), as well as the specter of a Bolshevik rebellion in Canada and the United States. When the Winnipeg General Strike erupted on May 15, 1919, the anti-Communist crusade and attending xenophobia were at their height. Consequently, there was suspicion and resentment of a long list of real and imagined undesirables, including socialists, radicals, enemy aliens, Bolshevists, Reds, Marxists, foreign agitators, revolutionaries, reactionaries, extremists and anarchists.

World War I and its aftermath also caused problems in Canada. With a population of fewer than 8 million, the nation had sent more than 600,000 men and women to the Western Front. After four years of fighting, approximately 67,000 soldiers had been killed, with one-third missing in action, and 173,000 wounded. Many soldiers had also broken under the strain of warfare and succumbed to post-traumatic stress disorder, described at the time as "nerve cases." Hundreds had even resorted to self-injury to avoid frontline action.

By the time the Armistice occurred, war-weary and grieving Canadians were understandably relieved to see the end of the casualty lists that had been published with grim regularity for four years in their daily newspapers and the ambulance trains returning uniformed servicemen on crutches, stretchers and wheelchairs. Added to the war dead and injured were thousands more, mostly between the ages of twenty and fifty, who from the autumn of 1918 to the spring of 1919 died mysteriously from the Spanish flu. Eventually, this bewildering pandemic took the lives of fifty thousand Canadians.

After World War I ended on November 11, 1918, thousands of soldiers began streaming home from European battlefields. The vast majority was eager to take part in stand-down ceremonies, march off from a final parade and return to civilian life. However, their transition into postwar society and the workplace was not always seamless. Many who were physically handicapped and emotionally traumatized by their war experience underwent a difficult and stressful readjustment to civilian life, and those unable to find work inevitably became frustrated and discontented.

Unemployed and unemployable veterans were particularly angry with "slackers" and "shirkers" who had not fought in the war and now appeared to be working in good jobs, as well as "foreigners" or "aliens" who had slipped in during the soldiers' absence overseas and taken employment away from "genuine" Canadians. Also, having fought for democracy, freedom and justice, many battle-hardened ex-servicemen returned with idealistic expectations of a better world. Instead, following demobilization, they faced the unsettling socioeconomic reality of postwar Canada. With demoralization, boredom and anger came the possibility of extreme action by the swelling ranks of jobless veterans.

Economic problems also followed the end of hostilities. The change from wartime to peacetime had come in the midst of galloping inflation, spiralling prices and high cost of living. Given a labour market gutted by demobilization, unemployment, especially among returned soldiers, was severe. In addition to lack of work and low wages, there were also complaints from veterans about the shortage of housing and lack of social assistance. At the same time, farmers' protests over falling wheat prices went largely ignored by the federal government. The result of this topsy-turvy economic situation was an atmosphere of financial uncertainty in the country.

Additionally, despite the official end of war, government censorship, orders-in-council and jailing of political prisoners continued for several months. As frustrated workers attempted to take economic control of the situation, there was widespread industrial unrest in the form of ongoing strikes and lockouts and a movement to organize all Canadian workers into the One Big Union (OBU). This, in turn, worried employers, business leaders, politicians and the nation's intelligence-gathering and security apparatus. Extremely concerned with the troublesome and violent-prone members of the Industrial Workers of the World (IWW) and the yet-to-be-formed OBU, the Canadian government increased surveillance on dozens of labour leaders and socialists.

Finally, two events occurred in the United States during the first half of 1919 that exacerbated concern over extremist activity and added to the fear of Bolshevism. In the first week of February, a general strike in Seattle, Washington, by sixty thousand militant workers and their supporters erupted but was quickly crushed by the city's Red-baiting mayor, Ole Hanson. Then, in June, an ambitious bombing campaign aimed at government officials by so-called Red agitators took place in eight American cities. The assassination attempt that received the most national press happened in Washington, D.C. There a bomb planted by a Philadelphia "anarchist" exploded, killing its carrier rather than its intended victim: United States attorney general A. Mitchell Palmer.

In the midst of this turbulent atmosphere, on May 1, 1919, Winnipeg's two thousand building trades workers, followed the next day by three thousand metal tradesmen of six separate unions, struck for higher wages and union recognition. Five days later, the Winnipeg Trades and Labor Council (WTLC) authorized a strike vote of more than twelve thousand members in sympathy with the building and metal trades workers. On May 7, the WTLC began distributing strike ballots to the Council's one hundred affiliated unions.

Despite the fact that more than five thousand metal trades and construction workers and their employers were careening towards a catastrophe, Liberal Premier T.C. Norris and Winnipeg's mayor Charles Gray took few steps to prevent the impending crisis and did not attempt conciliation until May 12. However, their last-minute efforts proved unsuccessful, largely because the three "ironmasters"—owners of Vulcan Iron Works, Manitoba Bridge and Iron Works and Dominion Bridge Company—refused to recognize the metal workers' year-old Metal Trades Council.

On the evening of May 13, the WTLC executive convened a meeting of several hundred trade unionists in the Labor Temple to announce the results of the strike vote. More than 11,000 ballots had been cast in favour and fewer than 500 opposed. The police had voted 149 to 11 for the strike and the firemen 149 to 6. The voting was much closer among printing pressmen with a tally of 50 to 21. From the vote, it was clear that the idea of using a general sympathetic strike to support the building construction and metal tradesmen was endorsed by Winnipeg's unionized workers.

Soon after the tally was announced, WTLC president James Winning made it official: the strike would begin on Thursday, May 15, at 11:00 a.m. During the day on May 14, Mayor Gray and Premier Norris unsuccessfully made further efforts to avoid the strike. Late that evening and in the presence of Manitoba's attorney general Thomas H. Johnson, Gray telephoned Winning requesting that the strike be delayed. "If the iron workers will agree tonight to concede your demands will the strike be abandoned?" asked Gray. "Well it might help but it is too late to discuss that now," replied Winning. Following the conversation, Gray telegraphed Acting Prime Minister Sir Thomas White in Ottawa, requesting "[f]ullest co-operation required toward effecting early settlement [of the strike]."

The walkout began the next day, with opposing sides offering very different views of its cause. The WTLC's Strike Committee insisted that legitimate demands for union recognition and wages caused the walkout; the Citizens' Committee of One Thousand (hereafter "Citizens"; occasionally, "1,000" is used in sources), representing the city's professional and business interests, asserted that the aim of the strike was revolution. A bitter struggle ensued, with both sides promoting their interpretation through special strike-edition newspapers. When the city's three daily newspapers began republishing after being temporarily suspended by the Strike Committee, they fully supported the Citizens.

SETTING THE SCENE

To become a newspaperman you need the hide of a dinosaur, the stamina of a Chinese coolie, the wakefulness and persistence of a mosquito, the analytical powers of a detective and the digging capacity of a steam shovel.
—*Roy Greenaway,* The News Game *(1966)*

JOURNALISTS

Samuel Hopkins Adams (1871–1958)

Born in Dunkirk, New York, in 1891, Adams became a reporter for the *New York Sun*. He later joined *McClure's Magazine* and then *Collier's Weekly*. In 1905, he wrote a series of articles for *Collier's* exposing many of the false claims of patent medicines and as a result developed a reputation as a "muckraker." He continued reporting for the *New York Sun* until 1929, and between 1920 and 1955, he authored more than a dozen short stories, novels and nonfiction works. Adams died in Beaufort, North Carolina, on November 15, 1958.

Benjamin Batsford (1892–1977)

Born in Minneapolis, Minnesota, Batsford served in France for Canada during World War I. In October 1918, he returned from overseas and rejoined the *Free Press* as an editorial cartoonist and reporter. He testified in the preliminary hearing of the Winnipeg strike trials. From 1921 until 1926, he drew a Canadian comic strip variously called *Unk and Billy* and *Billy's Uncle* and, in 1927, moved to the United States, where he continued a career in comic strips. In 1939, he was living in Garden City, New York, and working on Edgar Bergen's *Mortimer and Charlie* strip. During World War II, he created weekly editorial cartoons depicting the war. In 1945, Batsford retired from cartooning and moved to Long Island, New York, where he died on February 11, 1977.

Arthur Caylor (1890–1963)

Born in Kansas, Caylor moved with his family to Oregon at an early age and, in 1915, became a member of the first graduating class of Portland's Reed College. After graduation, he worked for the *Portland Telegram*, served as a sergeant in World War I and joined the *Winnipeg Tribune* in 1918 as a reporter. He moved to San Francisco in 1929 and began a lengthy career with the *San Francisco News* as a police and court reporter. In 1932, he started a column with the *News* that he would go on to write for more than thirty years. Caylor died in San Francisco on June 8, 1963.

John J. Conklin (1868–1952)

Born in Forest, Ontario, Conklin came to Winnipeg from Hamilton with his family in 1881. He entered the University of Manitoba in 1885 and wrote for the school's paper, *The Manitoban*. In 1886, he left university to work for the *Manitoba Free Press*. Over the next fifty-one years, he held several positions at the paper, including general reporter; music, drama and movie critic; telegraph, automobile and city editor; and editorial writer. He was also a freelance writer for several Canadian, American and British newspapers; Western correspondent for the *Canadian Moving Picture Digest*; and editor of the *Victoria Beach Herald*. Conklin retired in 1937 but continued to contribute articles to the *Free Press* until his death in Winnipeg on February 7, 1952.

John Conklin (sitting at left, in dark vest) in the *Manitoba Free Press*, July 1914. *Courtesy of Archives of Manitoba N2354, Foote 1381.*

John W. Dafoe (1866–1940)

Born in Combermere, Ontario, Dafoe joined the *Montreal Daily Herald* in 1883 and was appointed the paper's parliamentary reporter. Two years later, he became the founding editor of the *Ottawa Evening Journal* but left the paper in 1888 to join the *Manitoba Free Press*. In 1892, he retraced his steps east and spent several years at the *Montreal Herald*. Finally, in 1901, he returned to the *Free Press* as editor in chief, a position he held until 1944. He became one of the country's most influential and powerful journalists and wrote biographies of Prime Minister Sir Wilfrid Laurier and *Free Press* owner Clifford Sifton. Dafoe died in Winnipeg on January 9, 1944.

Frederick Dixon (1881–1931)

Born in Englefield, England, Dixon came in 1903 to Canada, where he trained as a draftsman and worked as an engraver. He was elected to the Manitoba legislature in 1915 as a Labour member for Centre Winnipeg. In the legislature, he forced an investigation into corruption by the government of Sir Rodmond Roblin, leading to his resignation as premier. After *Western Labor News* editor William Ivens was arrested during the Winnipeg General Strike, Dixon became the paper's co-editor with James Woodsworth. Dixon was tried for seditious libel in early 1920 but defended himself and was found not guilty. He was reelected to the Manitoba legislature in 1920 but resigned in 1923 due to ill health. Dixon died in Winnipeg on March 18, 1931.

Arthur M. Evans (1874–1967)

Born in Glinton, Northamptonshire, England, Evans came to the United States with his parents at the age of ten. He obtained his first newspaper job in Ironwood, Michigan, in 1899, and a year later, he moved to Chicago to work for the City Press Association. In 1901, he joined the *Chicago Chronicle* and in 1903 moved to the *Chicago Herald*, for which he worked for fifteen years. After joining the *Chicago Tribune* in 1918, his first overseas assignment was to cover the Paris Peace Conference and accompany President Woodrow Wilson on his tour of France, England and Italy. Evans remained with the *Tribune* for thirty-two years, serving as a political editor, legislative reporter, economics writer and travelling correspondent. He retired in 1950 and in 1959 was named Press Veteran of the Year by the Chicago Press Veterans Association. Evans died in St. Petersburg, Florida, on August 6, 1967.

James H. Hare (1856–1956)

Born in England, Hare was active as a photojournalist with *Collier's Weekly* from 1898 to 1914 and *Leslie's Weekly* from 1914 to 1922. He was the leading photographer during the Spanish-American and Russo-Japanese Wars, Mexican Revolution, First Balkan War and World War I. He photographed the aftermath of the 1908 San Francisco earthquake, the Wright brothers' early test flights and the 1917 Halifax Explosion in Nova Scotia, Canada. After 1922, Hare did little photography but lectured regularly. He retired in

1939 and was named the honorary president of the Overseas Press Club. Hare died in Teaneck, New Jersey, on June 24, 1956.

William Ivens (1878–1956)

Born in Barford, Warwickshire, England, Ivens came to Canada in 1896 and settled in Winnipeg in 1902. He attended the University of Manitoba as a ministerial candidate and in 1916 became minister of Winnipeg's McDougal Church. He broke with the church over his pacifism in 1917 and in August 1918 was appointed editor of the *Western Labor News*, the weekly paper of the Winnipeg Trades and Labor Council. During the strike, he was the editor of the *Western Labor News'* daily *Strike Bulletin* until his arrest for seditious conspiracy. After a trial in early 1920, he was found guilty and sentenced to a year in prison. While in jail, he was elected to the Manitoba legislature as a Labour member and was reelected in 1922 and 1927. In 1925, Ivens began a successful chiropractic practice in Winnipeg. He was defeated in the 1933 federal election and never held office again. Ivens died in Chula Vista, California, in 1956.

William Ivens, circa 1921.
Courtesy of Archives of Manitoba N10452.

William Main Johnson (1887–1959)

Born in Hamilton, Ontario, Johnson[1] showed an early interest in journalism by writing and selling his own weekly paper at age seven. After graduating with an honours degree in English and history from the University of Toronto, he joined the *Star* as a full-time cub reporter. In 1912, he became principal private secretary to Newton Rowell, president of the wartime Privy Council in Prime Minister Borden's Union government, and later a member of the Imperial War Cabinet in London, England. In late 1918, Johnson returned to Canada and rejoined the *Star*. He testified in the preliminary hearing of the Winnipeg strike trials. For the next twenty-six years, he remained with the paper in a succession of writing and executive editorial positions, including parliamentary reporter, circulation promotion and picture editor, director of the *Star*'s radio station (CFCA), *Star Weekly* editor, financial editor and editor in chief of the editorial page. In 1946, he became a business consultant and freelance journalist for Canadian, British and American publications. Johnson died in Toronto on December 11, 1959.

John Frederick Bligh Livesay (1875–1944)

Born in the Isle of Wight, Livesay came to Canada at the age of twenty. He began his Canadian journalism career in Winnipeg at twenty-eight with the *Winnipeg Tribune* and later joined the *Winnipeg Telegram*. After Western Associated Press (WAP) was established in September 1907, he became the agency's first general manager and continued in this position until September 1, 1917, when the association merged with the Central Provinces and the Eastern Press Association to become the national news-gathering service of Canadian Press (CP) Limited. After the merger, Livesay was appointed CP's assistant general manager and placed in charge of the Winnipeg bureau and western Canadian operations. During World War I, he also acted as dominion censor for the West and spent several months overseas as a war correspondent. In 1920, he left Winnipeg to become general manager of CP in Toronto and continued in this position until he retired in 1939. Livesay died in Clarkson, Ontario, on June 15, 1944, and in 1974 was inducted into the Canadian News Hall of Fame.

Knox Magee (1877–1934)

Born in Grenville, Ontario, Magee began his journalistic career in 1896 in Philadelphia, Pennsylvania. Returning to Canada, he was successively editor of the humorous publication *The Moon*, editorial writer on the *Toronto Globe* and managing editor of the *Saturday Post*. After moving to Winnipeg, he initially worked as an editorial writer on the *Winnipeg Tribune* before assuming similar duties with the *Winnipeg Saturday Post*. In December 1917, he became general manger and editor of the *Winnipeg Telegram* and remained with the paper until September 19, 1919. Magee died in Winnipeg on May 9, 1934.

John J. Moncrieff (1865–1939)

Born in Scalloway in the Shetlands, Moncrieff came to Canada at ten with his family, who located in St. Andrews, Manitoba. In 1879, with W.T. Thompson and four other men, Moncrieff founded the *Winnipeg Daily News*. When the *Daily News* was merged into the *Winnipeg Sun*, Moncrieff joined the paper. After the *Manitoba Free Press* purchased the *Winnipeg Sun*, he worked briefly for the paper. In 1890, he became news editor of the *Winnipeg Tribune* and the paper's managing editor in 1903. After the Southam family acquired the *Winnipeg Tribune* in 1920, he was appointed associate editor, a position he held until retirement in 1936. Moncrieff died in Winnipeg on April 11, 1939.

William R. Plewman (1880–1963)

Born in Bristol, England, Plewman moved to Canada with his parents when he was eight. He left public school at thirteen and went to work as a messenger boy and proofreader at the Methodist Bookroom in Toronto. He considered becoming a lawyer and spent four years in a law office, but in 1898, he became a cub reporter on the *Toronto News*. Four years later, he joined the *Star*, and except for a fifteen-month period between 1912 and 1914, he remained with the paper for fifty-five years. During the two world wars, he wrote the paper's celebrated "War Reviewed" column. Plewman continued with the *Toronto Star* as an editorial writer and columnist until he retired in 1955. He died in Toronto on September 24, 1963.

Garnet C. Porter (1866–1945)

Born in Russellville, Kentucky, Porter came to Canada in 1900, leaving behind an adventure-filled past as a legal counsel, Kentucky outlaw and feudist (where he earned the title "Colonel"), soldier of fortune and Yukon prospector. Settling in Toronto, he entered newspaper work and developed into an ace reporter for the *Toronto World*. In 1904, he became editor in chief of the *Calgary Eye Opener* and, two years later, joined the *Winnipeg Telegram*, for which he was successively news editor, managing editor and editor in chief. The Colonel left the paper in 1916 to start his own news service, Porter's International Press News Bureau. He also did freelance reporting for several Canadian newspapers, including the *Montreal Star* and *Toronto Evening Telegram*. When the *Winnipeg Telegram* merged with the rival *Winnipeg Tribune* in October 1920, he joined the new paper. He ended his journalistic career as a columnist for the Saturday *Tribune* supplement and freelance writer specializing in crime stories for American detective magazines. Porter died in Winnipeg on March 6, 1945.

Charles Roland (1869–1936)

Born in St. Catharines, Ontario, in 1869, Roland came to Manitoba in 1889 but soon left the city. After working in Victoria and Cleveland, he returned to Winnipeg in 1903 and engaged in journalism and trade papers. In 1907, he was appointed commissioner of the Winnipeg Development and Industrial Bureau, a position he held for thirteen years. In 1914, he was chosen as secretary of the International exhibition held in Winnipeg. During World War I, he was also secretary of the Manitoba Patriotic Fund and Winnipeg organizer of the Victory Loan Drive. After 1920, Roland left Winnipeg for the west coast but later returned to become manager of Winnipeg's Employers' Association and the Better Business Bureau. Roland died in Winnipeg on August 22, 1936.

Mary Dawson Snider (1870–1932)

Born in Lambton, Ontario, Mary Adelaide Dawson joined the *Toronto Evening Telegram* in 1901. In her early years, she wrote columns in the women's pages, acted as secretary to proprietor/publisher John Ross Robertson and became the daily's first female reporter. She was one of the original members of the Canadian Women's Press Club when it was formed on June 24, 1904, and also one of the founders of the Toronto Women's Press Club. In 1908, she married one of the paper's senior editors, C.H. Jerry Snider. Her most famous scoop was in April 1912, when she met and interviewed survivors of the *Titanic* disaster by posing as a nurse and slipping through a waterfront police cordon. During World War I, she was in charge of the female workers in a Toronto munitions plant. She continued with the *Toronto Telegram* until the late 1920s and during this time also contributed to *Saturday Night*, *Canadian Magazine* and *Canadian Countryman* magazine. Snider died in Toronto on September 3, 1932.

Fletcher Sparling (1875–1958)

Born on his father's farm in Grey County, Ontario, Fletcher Sparling went to work at sixteen for Simpson's in Toronto. He left in 1893 for the R.H. White Company in Boston, and for the next eighteen years, he worked in the United States as a salesman, department buyer, merchandise manager and merchant. In 1911, he became store manager of Goodwin's Limited in Montreal. On May 2, 1915, he moved to Winnipeg to accept the position of general manager of the Hudson's Bay Company (HBC) store. He remained

Fletcher Sparling, 1921. *Courtesy of Hudson's Bay Company Archives, Archives of Manitoba.*

in this position until August 15, 1921, when he assumed the management of HBC operations in Calgary. However, a disagreement over his replacement resulted in his resignation from the HBC on July 5, 1923. Sparling died in Vancouver on March 31, 1958.

W.A. T. Sweatman (1879–1941)

Born in Pembroke, Ontario, William Andrew Travers Sweatman was educated in Manitoba and received a BA (1900) and MA (1903) from St. John's College. He read law with F.H. Phippen and Isaac Pitblado. Sweatman was called to the Manitoba Bar in 1906 and was associated from 1912 to 1939 with the firm of Richards, Sweatman, Kemp and Fillmore. In 1910, he married Constance Newton, the daughter of Winnipeg pioneer Charles Henry Newton. In 1916, he represented builder Thomas Kelly in litigation over the construction of the Manitoba legislative buildings. He was a member of the Crown's legal team assembled to prosecute the strike leaders during the 1919 and 1920 trials. Sweatman was created a KC in 1920. From 1921 to 1925, he was the president of the Winnipeg Board of Trade. In 1938, he ran unsuccessfully for mayor of Winnipeg. Sweatman moved to Toronto to practice law and died there on September 8, 1941.

James S. Woodsworth (1874–1942)

Born near Toronto, Ontario, Woodsworth moved with his family to Brandon, Manitoba, in 1882. He was ordained a Methodist minister in 1896 and in 1902 took a position as minister of Grace Church in Winnipeg. In 1907, he was appointed superintendent of All People's Church in Winnipeg's North End. During World War I, he opposed conscription and in 1918 resigned from the Methodist Church over this issue. He returned to Winnipeg during the strike, and when *Western Labor News* editor William Ivens was arrested, Woodsworth joined Fred Dixon to produce the strikers' paper. He was arrested for seditious libel in the final days of the strike but was never brought to trial. From 1921 to 1942, he represented Winnipeg North as a member of Parliament. During this time, he helped establish the federal Co-operative Commonwealth Federation (CCF) Party, which later became the New Democratic Party. Woodsworth died in Vancouver, British Columbia, on March 21, 1942.

MAJOR FIGURES, ORGANIZATIONS AND LOCATIONS

Alfred Andrews KC—lawyer, executive member of the Citizens' Committee

Roger Bray—veteran and leader of the pro-strike returned soldiers

City Hall—located at the corner of Main Street and William Avenue

"enemy aliens"—Winnipeg's twenty-seven thousand registered Eastern European immigrants

Charles Gray—Winnipeg mayor

Industrial Bureau/Board of Trade—Citizens' Committee of One Thousand (1,000) headquarters

"ironmasters"—owners of Vulcan Iron Works, Manitoba Bridge and Iron Works and Dominion Bridge Company

City Hall and Union Bank building, 1919. *Courtesy of Gary Becker Collection, Heritage Winnipeg.*

Mayor Charles Gray, circa 1920. *Courtesy of Archives of Manitoba N20991.*

IWW—Industrial Workers of the World, an American revolutionary trade union formed in 1905

Thomas H. Johnson—Manitoba attorney general

Brigadier General H.D.B. Ketchen—commanding officer, Military District No. 10

Labor Temple—Strike Committee headquarters

Donald MacPherson—Winnipeg police chief

Main Street and Portage Avenue—Winnipeg's main intersection

Market Square—a large square behind City Hall

Arthur Meighen, circa 1920. *Courtesy of Archives of Manitoba N9465.*

Arthur Meighen—acting minister of justice, Government of Canada

Thomas C. Norris—Manitoba premier

OBU—One Big Union, a Canadian syndicalist trade union founded in June 1919

Aylesworth B. Perry—commissioner, Royal North West Mounted Police

"returned soldiers"—Winnipeg's fifteen thousand demobilized World War I veterans

Senator Gideon Robertson—minister of labour, Government of Canada

Charles Roland—secretary, Manitoba Patriotic Fund

Robert B. Russell—leading member of the Strike Committee

Fletcher Sparling—general manager, Hudson's Bay Company

Cortlandt Starnes—superintendent, Winnipeg Royal North West Mounted Police

Stoney Mountain Penitentiary—federal prison north of Winnipeg

Travers Sweatman—lawyer, executive member of the Citizens' Committee

Victoria Park—large park near the Labor Temple, where workers and returned soldiers gathered during the strike; the park was renamed Soldiers' Parliament during the strike

James Winning—president, Winnipeg Trades and Labor Council

WTLC—Winnipeg Trades and Labor Council, representing twelve thousand unionized workers

CHAPTER 1
A CLOAK FOR SOMETHING FAR DEEPER

MAY 15–18

On May 15 at exactly 7:00 a.m., the Winnipeg general sympathetic strike began at Manitoba Telephone when dozens of the province's operators started leaving the city's five phone exchanges. By day's end, five hundred "Hello Girls" had abandoned their switchboards. At 11:00 a.m., thousands of men and women left the city's factories, offices, hotels, breweries, distilleries, warehouses and print shops. Joined by hundreds of curiosity seekers, the strikers converged downtown. Large crowds assembled first near City Hall and then south along Main Street to the city's busiest intersection at Portage Avenue.

With streetcars soon out of service, the city's public transportation system ceased to function. Bread, milk and ice deliveries were halted; building elevators stopped running; and the city's water pressure in buildings was reduced to only first-floor use. With the exception of a few management officials, federal postal employees went home, and before long, restaurants, barbershops and theatres were closed. Firemen abandoned their stations, and city police threatened to walk off the job but were kept on duty at the request of the Strike Committee. By the end of the day, as many as eighteen thousand non-unionized workers had spontaneously joined twelve thousand striking WTLC members.

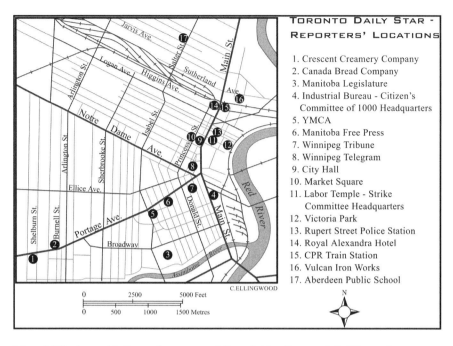

Map of Winnipeg with *Toronto Star* reporters' "beat." *Map Courtesy of C. Ellingwood.*

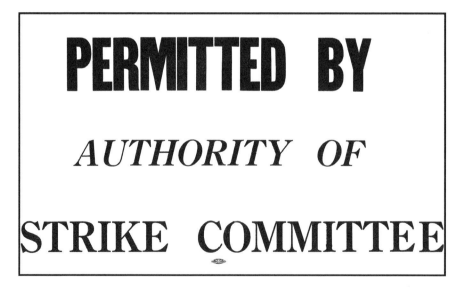

Strike Committee Permit Card, May 16. *Courtesy of Archives of Manitoba N488, Winnipeg Strike 2.*

Fire department volunteers during the strike. *Courtesy of Archives of Manitoba N2736, Foote 1670.*

In order to maintain bread, milk and ice deliveries, as well as allow restaurants and movie theatres to remain open, representatives of the Strike Committee and City Council agreed on May 16 to have these businesses display twelve- by sixteen-inch cards indicating "Permitted by Authority of Strike Committee." In other developments, Brigadier General H.D.B. Ketchen, commanding officer of Military District No. 10, which included

Winnipeg, informed the Great War Veterans Association (GWVA) that all troops in the city had been notified that they were on duty and must not leave the armouries or barracks. He also recruited a returned soldier to infiltrate the Strike Committee. Union workers who made and finished metal printing plates and operated the web printing presses at the city's three daily newspapers voted to join the general strike the next day. On the same day, *Collier's* magazine correspondent Samuel Hopkins Adams likely arrived in Winnipeg.

One hour after the next day's noon closure of the *Manitoba Free Press*, *Winnipeg Telegram* and *Winnipeg Tribune*, more than two hundred commercial and brokerage telegraphers walked off their jobs. Among the wire service men who abandoned their keys were the five unionized operators at the Winnipeg bureau of Canadian Press (CP) news service. With the city now in a virtual communications blackout, two daily strike papers appeared: the pro-strike *Western Labor News* and the anti-strike *Winnipeg Citizen*. The next day, Mayor Gray announced that despite his personal efforts and those of Premier Norris and other representative bodies, no settlement had been achieved. To reassure citizens, Gray announced that both sides in the strike were working to keep law and order and that water, milk, general food supply and fire and police protection would continue to be provided to the public. On May 18, *Toronto Star* reporter William Main Johnson arrived in Winnipeg.

Veteran Winnipeg freelance reporter Garnet Porter began supplying news to the outside world on day one of the strike.[2] His first of more than fifty dispatches to Canadian daily newspapers appeared in the *Vancouver Province*. In a front-page story headlined "Twenty-Seven Thousand Employees Out on Sympathetic Strike," Porter raised the threat of aliens in the dispute. "The Manitoba Free Press points to this phase of the case and evidently having in view the thousands of alien enemies in North Winnipeg says: 'There are unruly and criminal elements in Winnipeg as the current records of courts show…Everyone who knows this city and gives thought to the matter is aware that this is not an overstatement of fact.'"

The next day, he mentioned another danger. "A menacing phase of the situation was the handing to each striker as he left the C.P.R. shops a number of pamphlets issued by the Socialist party and copies of the Socialist Bulletin." By May 18, he was referring to the strike as a "state of siege" and reporting that "conditions are operating to increase the unrest and general impatience…Winnipeg is…ready to take control of lawlessness should any develop…General Ketchen has 7000 returned soldiers at his disposal in the event of martial law being declared."

In the same dispatch, Porter commented on the suspension of the city's daily press. "In many reports the closing of the city's daily papers has increased the danger of the situation, because wild rumors are freely circulated and careless talk is flamed into menacing threats." Despite conceding that "[o]rder prevails at strike headquarters and many returned soldiers are among the strikers," he added, "though there are among them many alien enemies." He ended the dispatch by mentioning the use of special constables to deal with disorder. "A suggestion from business men to Mayor Gray that 800 special constables be sworn in did not meet with his approval though the mayor is on the job and has issued a public statement threatening swift punishment for any lawless act."

The first issue of the strikers' daily paper, the *Western Labor News*, appeared on May 17. In "Why the General Strike," the paper's editor, William Ivens, explained the reason for the walkout.

> *Winnipeg is gripped by the biggest strike in its history. Why? Simply because a few employers refuse to recognize the right of Labor to organize. After repeated efforts to have them act in a reasonable manner the men in the Metal Trades struck work to enforce their demands. The Building Trades Council was recognized by the Employers' Association, and their demands were declared to be just and reasonable, but the employers said that those reasonable wages could not be paid. Or, in other words the men involved must work for less than a living wage. If the workers must starve it may as well be now as later. This is the reason behind the General Strike.*

Then Ivens named the strike's opponents. "Opposed to these forces is the small but well organized force of the bosses of industries. They have wealth and the government behind them. They own the wholesale house, etc., etc. They say they will fight to the last ditch. They will not yield except under dire compulsion. Their agents are everywhere and they know everything."

The following day, in the first issue of the *Winnipeg Citizen*, the paper's editor[3] offered a very different interpretation of events. First he explained the need for the paper.

> *This newspaper is issued because of the unquestionable necessity for placing before the great body of the citizens of Winnipeg the actual facts of the strike situation from the standpoint of the citizens themselves and in*

order adequately to inform them of the issue that faces Winnipeg in this, the most serious hour of her history. It must be stated at the outset that this publication is not issued on behalf of the workers, nor on behalf of the employers, nor in opposition to either of them as such, but simply and solely in the interests of the hundred and fifty thousand or more non-participants in the issues which served as the cause of the strike—or as the excuses for it. It is issued only on behalf of the great mass of the public which is suffering from the strike's effects.

Next he asserted the strike's real purpose. "It is to the general public of Winnipeg that we speak, in stating without equivocation that this is not a strike at all, in the ordinary sense of the term—it is Revolution. It is a serious attempt to overturn British institutions in this Western country and to supplant them with the Russian Bolshevik system of Soviet rule…Let us repeat—this is not a strike; it is just plain, ugly revolution."

From a lengthy story in *Collier's* titled "The One Big Union" and subtitled "What the 'Strike' at Winnipeg Really Showed," it is likely that correspondent Samuel Hopkins Adams arrived in Winnipeg during the first few days of the strike and remained until June 14.[4] The magazine's editor accompanied Hopkins's article with a front-page box notice.

Although Winnipeg's general sympathetic strike has been called off, its significance its bearing upon future strike methods, are still of tremendous importance. According to many newspapers, the Winnipeg affair masked an attempt to establish a soviet form of government in America. Samuel Hopkins Adams, who is considered one of the most accurate reporters in America, could not find any justification for this charge against the Winnipeg strikers. But the fact, and the formidable fact, that he did find was the power of the O.B.U—the One Big Union. More articles by Mr. Adams on the labor situation will appear in Collier's—The Editor.

In analyzing the strike's development, Hopkins reported on claims by Citizens that the Strike Committee was Bolshevist. "A Central Strike Committee was formed to run the strike. Locally and in dispatches this committee has been described as a soviet exercising a Bolshevist control of city government…A soviet is a positive establishment of a form of government. There has been nothing of the sort accomplished in Winnipeg up to date. And all the official utterances of the strikers have been anti-soviet and anti-revolution."

He also commented on similar allegations against Ivens and the *Western Labor News*.

> *The one specific charge, identifying the tie-up as a Bolshevist movement, I have carefully investigated. It is brought by the Committee of One Thousand and in its official organ, the "Winnipeg Citizen," which publishes an alleged quotation from the "Western Labor News," the organ of the strike, in which the Rev. William Ivens, its editor, appear as having said at a Victoria park meeting on May 16: "Winnipeg is now governed by a soviet; the seat of authority has been transferred from the City hall to the Labor Temple." No such statement ever appeared in the "Western Labor News" nor anything even approximating it. Mr. Ivens states unequivocally that he made no such statement. Men of good character, present at the meeting, state that he did not. As to the misquotation from the "Western Labor News," a representative of the Committee of One Thousand has admitted to me that this was a "mistake." I have no doubt that it was honestly made in the haste of the campaign. But that, having been discovered and confirmed, it should not have been corrected is little to the committee's credit…there is no utterance or announcement of the labor element which indicates a soviet plan. On the contrary, the official organ and the official speakers have repeatedly declared that "what we do not want" is revolution and the soviet.*

Finally, Hopkins reported that the One Big Union was involved in the walkout.

> *But the "O.B.U.," the One Big Union, is in force and in operation here to-day. Those leaders who deny it are seeking to deny the obvious. Those who, tacitly admitting it, say that it developed of itself out of the logic of events, are nearer the truth. It is a fact, and a formidable fact, pregnant with possibilities which extend even to revolution…It is in form and essence the general sympathetic strike…Yet it can paralyze a city. Expanded, it could paralyze a nation.*

MAY 19–23

On May 19, regular bread and milk deliveries continued with strikers' permit signs on the rigs, hospitals were properly equipped and the Police Court operated as usual, with fewer arrests than normal. The *Citizen* was available at

Strikers massed at Victoria Park. *Courtesy of Archives of Manitoba N2745, Foote 1679.*

fire halls and the Industrial Bureau and the *Labor News* at the Labor Temple and on the streets. The post office remained closed, with mail piled up at the depots in and outside the city; gasoline was shut off; and water remained at low pressure. The electric lights were maintained by order of the Strike Committee, which also established a censorship on all press dispatches emanating from Winnipeg. False alarms kept Citizens volunteer firefighters busy, and train service alone prevented absolute isolation for the city.

On May 20, Citizens representatives led by executive member Alfred Andrews spoke at a special City Council meeting to explain the organization's purpose. At the same time, there was a mass meeting of the GWVA. The next day, normal water pressure resumed after volunteers wrested control from city workers. Representatives of two of the city's three ironmasters met with Mayor Gray and City Council. During the evening, a train carrying Minister of Labour Gideon Robertson and Minister of Justice Arthur Meighen from Ottawa to Winnipeg was intercepted in Fort William (now Thunder Bay) by a Citizens delegation.

On May 22, Robertson and Meighen arrived in Winnipeg and announced that the strike was a "cloak for an effort to overturn proper authority." On the same day, *Toronto Telegram* reporter Mary Dawson Snider and *Toronto Star* reporter William R. Plewman arrived in Winnipeg. The *Free Press* resumed a limited publication and established communication with the outside world through a wireless telegraphy antenna installed and operated from a tower on the roof of the *Manitoba Free Press* building. An afternoon mass meeting of strikers and returned soldiers was held at Victoria Park, and the permit signs on bread, milk and ice rigs disappeared. Department stores made their first morning deliveries since the strike began, and City Council stopped the distribution of the *Citizen* at fire stations. More than twenty thousand sacks of mail were now held in the main post office, postal warehouse and in various stations. Mayor Gray was told by the ironmasters that the Citizens had requested them not to negotiate with the strikers. The Citizens hired the McDonald Detective Agency to provide private police services.

On May 23, Meighen, Robertson, General Ketchen, Premier Norris and Manitoba attorney general Johnson conferred at the Royal Alexandra Hotel. A late-night mediation meeting at City Hall attended by various stakeholders in the strike was convened by Mayor Gray, although Arthur Meighen and Gideon Robertson were absent. Manitoba Telephone resumed service with volunteer replacement workers, the Labor Café opened at the Strathcona Hotel to feed strikers and another mass meeting of strikers was held at Victoria Park. Striking federal postal employees were issued an ultimatum by Gideon Robertson to return to work by May 26 or permanently forfeit jobs and pensions.

Toronto Star correspondent Main Johnson reported the strike in a series of sixteen dispatches published between May 19 and May 26.[5] His first story on May 19 reported no shortage of speculation. "Especially in the absence of regular news channels there were all sorts of rumors rife in Winnipeg, some of the most disquieting nature, but no confirmation of any of them was available. One of the wildest was that Mayor Gray was to be deported and a full-fledged Soviet Government instituted."

He then addressed one of the strikers' main demands, the issue of union recognition.

> *It is felt by a lot of people who are not necessarily in sympathy with the strikers…that the employers have chosen a bad ground on which to fight. To these people, and there are many, it is incredible that a general strike at this time of day should be fought on the issue of recognition of the union. It reveals, they say, in the minds of the employers a backward or*

Toronto Star reporter William Main Johnson, 1917. *Courtesy of Toronto Public Library.*

at least a stationary look that is difficult to understand…Anyone studying labor conditions and labor throughout the world knows that compared with many doctrines and movements today, trade unionism is a conservative, constructive force…and from this point of view it seems strange that [Winnipeg] employers should not encourage unions and their recognition, rather than oppose them.

Meanwhile, the *Vancouver Province* continued with Porter's dispatches, which by now were conflating the strike with Soviet government. The *Province* headlined his May 19 story "'Red' Section of Winnipeg Strikers Proclaims Soviet Government in that City." "While the Soviet government was being proclaimed," wrote Porter, "the Citizens' Committee of One Thousand was in session at the Industrial bureau, with probably 500 autos stretched on street on blocks both sides…Perhaps the news of the soviet proceedings did cause some of the citizens to take a firmer grip on themselves and their jaws become a little more resolutely set."

More compliments from Porter for the Citizens followed.

While the strikers adopted resolutions and appointed committees for their opera bouffe,[6] municipal republic, the business men at [sic] industrial bureau "districted" the town, received offers of cars, completed lists of volunteers who would, on signal, call at designated points and pick up minute men and take them to certain points to co-operate with whatever force may be utilized to conduct the city's affairs in an emergency.

Also on May 19, Ivens explained in the *Daily Press* why the Strike Committee had halted publication of the city's three newspapers.

For the first time in history Winnipeg is without its Daily Press. The reason is clear. It sets out once again deliberately to misrepresent the case of the workers. A year ago we issued a strike bulletin to call their bluff and correct their misstatements…We do not think they like it but then, for nearly five years, they have been howling their heads off to suppress papers that told the truth—surely it is a case of simple justice at this time to muzzle for a few days the enemies of freedom and truth.

The next day, in "The Gagging of the Press," the *Citizen*'s editor rebutted Ivens's explanation.

THE WINNIPEG CITIZEN | EXTRA

Vol. 1   May 21, 1919.   Published in Winnipeg in the interest of the Citizens.   No. 3

Winnipeg is No Longer Living "By Authority of the Strike Committee"

THE authorities have taken adequate measures to enable you to go about your work and business in safety.

Workers are returning to their positions. Business houses are opening and the necessaries of life are again within the reach of the people.

The authorities assure you of adequate protection and advise you to go about business as usual.

The Strike Committee is no longer able to intimidate citizens and prevent them getting the necessaries of existence.

"Permission to Live" Cards Go

"Permission to Live" cards are being removed from bread and milk delivery wagons. The wave of resentment against Bolsheviki legends required on these conveyances, "Permitted by Authority of the Strike Committee," has caused the late temporary government at the Labor Temple to order these "yellow tickets" taken off.

Water pressure goes back to normal. At the request of the Citizen's Committee yesterday at the City Hall, City Council by a vote of 7 to 5 ordered that water pressure be returned to normal. Aldermen Heaps, Queen, Wigginton, Simpson and Robinson, the so-called labor men, voted against.

I.W.W. Ideals Don't Appeal to White Men

The tyranny of the five in control at the Labor Temple deprived us of bread, milk, fire protection, telegraph, telephone, mail and communication with the outside world. Is this your ideal of freedom and democratic government? Our opinions may differ about other problems of the day but we stand united against the I.W.W., Bolsheviki and Soviet Government.

"Let Us Settle the One Big Issue"

Is every individual dispute between employer and employe to continue to disrupt the life of the whole community?

Fly your flag and let none forget what it stands for!

As you walk to work "by permission of the Strike Committee" just think it over.

Winnipeg Citizen, May 21.

The stopping of the daily press is one of the worst things that has been done by the strikers…It enables the Labor News to print what it pleases and suppress what displeases it…It glories also in the suppression of the daily press "to prevent misrepresentation"—and yet the suppression of the press has permitted the most amazing circulation of rumors without any agency to stop them…The daily press was suppressed for telling the truth about the situation, and to enable the Strike Committee to tell what it liked to people at large…without fear of contradiction.

Winnipeg freelance reporter John Conklin wrote more than seventy dispatches on the strike.[7] One of his first stories appeared in the *Toronto Star* on May 21 under the headline "No Foreigners on Strike Committee."

A peculiar thing is that the Strike Committee in charge in Winnipeg are all, without exception, English or Canadians. Rev. Wm. Ivens is a Canadian, born in Middlesex County.[8] Alderman W.B. Simpson, former superintendent of the Free Press plant, a strong anti-war man, is a native of Hamilton, Ontario. He is the leader of the Labor Aldermen on the City Council, serving his fourth year. Alderman Queen, Alderman Ernest Robinson, the secretary, and President Winning, are Englishmen…There are no foreigners on the executive committee, and one and all claim they are saving the West from the Bolsheviki system now controlling Russia.

On the same day, Ivens offered strategic advice to strikers.

The only thing that the workers have to do to win the strike is to do nothing. Just eat, sleep, play, love, laugh and look at the sun. This is the greatest strike ever put on in Winnipeg and it can be made the greatest victory if every striker does absolutely nothing. Join the "do nothing" club and be a son of rest till the strike is over. It will not last long. You will have plenty of work when it is over. For the present in a lawful, orderly and perfectly constitutional way—do nothing.

By the time the *Free Press* began republishing on May 22, the paper's editor, John W. Dafoe, had become convinced that the strike was a revolution masterminded by OBU promoters, organized by local "Red" labour leaders seeking personal gain through a Soviet-style dictatorship and supported by Winnipeg's numerous enemy aliens. In the daily's first issues since being suspended five days earlier, he published three editorials.

John W. Dafoe, circa 1930s.
Courtesy of Archives of Manitoba
N19540.

"The Attempted Suppression of the Press" was Dafoe's main comment in the morning edition. The front-page editorial, emphasized with uppercase letters, attacked the strike.

> *The Free Press WAS NOT THE VICTIM OF THE GENERAL STRIKE movement. Nor was the Free Press sacrificed for the purpose of vindicating the right to "collective bargaining" by the worker….No, the Free Press was the POLITICAL VICTIM of the soviet government. It was "suppressed" by a ukase from the revolutionary head center because they did not like its views and feared its influence At The Moment When They Were Attempting Revolution. They recognized it as an obstacle to the success of the revolution.*

Next he identified who had "suppressed" the paper. "All this is in keeping with the doctrines and practices of Lenine and Trotsky, the High Priests of the Winnipeg Reds who were responsible for this conspiracy…

The Free Press submits its ease against these vain and foolish tyrants of an hour to the judgment of free people who know what liberty is and have no intention of exchanging their birthright for revolutionary nostrums imported from Moscow."

Dafoe then targeted Ivens's May 19 statement that "for nearly five years" Winnipeg's daily press had "been howling their heads off to suppress papers that told the truth."

> *There is no doubt about what those words mean. The five years during which the Free Press and other papers have been persecuting "papers that told the truth" are the five years covering the Great War. The papers whose woes were so keenly felt by our local galaxy of Reds, were the treasonable pro-German papers published in Canada and the still more dangerous sheets devoted to German propaganda which came in from outside. These were the only papers that were disturbed or suppressed during the war.*

Dafoe's second editorial, "Anarchists and Aliens," linked five members of the Strike Committee to the Russian Revolution and associated the strike with the OBU and foreigners.

> *It is through the solid fanatical allegiance of the Germans, Austrians, Huns and Russians in the labor unions that the Red Five—Russell, Veitch, Robinson, Ivens and Winning—have climbed to power in the labor organizations…The idea behind the One Big Union is to employ these masses of rough, uneducated foreigners, who know nothing of our customs and our civilization, to browbeat and over-ride the intelligent and skilled craftsmen of the more technical trades who are numerically weaker.*[9]

In the afternoon edition, Dafoe used "The Great Dream of the Winnipeg Soviet" to label the strike's leaders as plotters in a "conspiracy against the daily press." Once again, his target was Ivens.

> *The bright idea here was to give Rev. Wm. Ivens—the notorious pacifist—a good start with the daily which he has long yearned to publish by putting the regular dailies—which give employment to hundreds of workers—out of business. Mr. Ivens, who has been uplifted by his new associations to the point where he regards the commandments against stealing and covetousness as effete and reactionary ideas, was very busy last week expounding to his*

William Plewman, 1944. *Courtesy of GetStock/Toronto Star.*

cronies his great business idea which, in its practical application, was to commit mayhem on the daily press and while they were thus out of action to steal some of their business. Blood Bolshevist doctrine and practice this!

On the same day the *Free Press* republished, *Toronto Star* reporter William Plewman arrived in Winnipeg. He remained in the city until June 27 and during this time wrote over ninety dispatches, more than any visiting journalist. His first story appeared on May 23 under the headline "Outward Appearances Show No Sign of Any Big Strike." In this front-page report, he addressed the Bolshevism issue. "[The strikers] have gone pretty far and they have made some mistakes but they have not perpetrated Bolshevism… There is no Soviet. There was little or no terrorism. The city thus far…has been more orderly than for a similar period in years."

Plewman also met with Ivens to explain the strikers' actions. The interview, which appeared in the *Toronto Star*'s sister paper, the *Star Weekly*, began with Ivens denouncing rumors of violence and rioting in Winnipeg.

> *"I do not want to win the strike unless our cause is just. The world is hearing of bloodshed and rioting in Winnipeg that never had occurred,"* continued Ivens. *"There have been no cases in the Police Courts of striker disorder and there has been less crime in the last six days than at any time during the last six months." "Have you any fear that if the strike is prolonged or other incitements as you see them are offered, that the extreme or rowdy element will sweep away the present leadership?" "No, the men are keeping cool and taking our advice to win by simply doing nothing."*

Ivens then answered several questions.

> *"How about the unionizing of the firemen, police and waterworks employees? I understand you stood up for that move last year. Do you still think that justifiable and in the public interest?" "Certainly. It is the fundamental right of all workmen to organize and to gain their ends by constitutional means." "Is it legal for the postal employees to strike?" "Quite legitimate." "And what is the great ultimate?" "The substitution of the industrial system for profit by the industrial system for use." "Can you gain that by constitutional means?" "I think so. I am against violent means. If the strikers go wrong. If they insist on anything more than their rights,"* he declared in conclusion, *"I am prepared to fight them."*

Also on May 23, Mayor Charles Gray convened a round table conference at City Hall to bring together opposing sides and interested parties in the dispute. Plewman attended the evening meeting and described the event in "Might Have End with One Good Word." One of the most revealing exchanges he reported was between Citizens member Alfred Andrews and strike leader Bob Russell.

Mr. Andrews: The discussion has been very enlightening to me. Our object here is solution of a pressing problem. I am satisfied that there will be no negotiations, and that the strike will break unless the postal clerks go back, the firemen resume work and the policemen are well rooted in their positions. (Loud smile) Don't smile. It would be splendid diplomacy if you give assurances along that line before there are further defections from your ranks.

Mr. Russell: What's your idea?

Mr. Andrews: A number of sympathetic strikers are returning to their jobs. At 9 Monday morning [May 26] *the Government starts the postal service. There is no trouble getting any men. It has been demonstrated that volunteers can fight fires. They showed what could be done…Telephone girls have come to me crying. It is not necessary to get a definition of collective bargaining. That is going to be given. But when a man breaks into my garage and steals my car and gets into my house and takes my furniture, I am not going to bargain with him, until he makes redress.*

Mr. Russell: We have not broken into your house or stolen your car.

Mr. Andrews: No but you made the firemen, to whom we trust our lives, break the agreement not to strike before May 1920, almost before the ink was dry.

Mr. Russell: Made them?

Mr. Andrews: Well, permitted them. And I would lose everything I have rather than bargain with you before they return. Remember, you never lose anything by doing what's right…Public opinion is against you.

Mr. Russell: I hope you give us credit for understanding the basis of society. The feudal system is going…The workmen in their economic organizations say they are the producers of wealth. Withdraw labor and no more wealth is produced as we [the strikers] *have proved. Has not the workingman the same right to demand from you that you return the proportion of wealth that he creates? The trades unions say they are prepared to negotiate what shall be the working day and the hours of pay and then agree and sign. There never is a sympathy strike on the matter of pay, only on some principle…*

Toronto Telegram reporter Mary Dawson Snider (front row, second on left), 1904. *Courtesy of Library and Archives Canada PA-138844.*

> *The strike has proven to the workers that we can act in the industrial field to the extent of running against the State…We have defied authority, but have not recognized it from start to finish. Never from the start have our tactics been an attack on the State.*

The only visiting female reporter to cover the strike was the *Toronto Telegram*'s Mary Dawson Snider. She arrived in Winnipeg on May 22 and remained until June 10. During this time, she wrote fourteen dispatches. In her first story, she reported developments at Citizens headquarters. "They have…between six and seven thousand sworn in for military duty to maintain law and order. They can be mobilized and rushed to any point by car." She also cast doubt about police loyalty. "They [officers] have been left on duty," but citizens "very much doubt the outcome if things came to a test." Finally, by quoting a non-striking returned soldier, she associated the strike with Bolshevism. "I fought the Bolsheviki in Europe. I'll be damned if I will help them here."

Fred Dixon, MLA, circa
1921. *Courtesy of Archives of
Manitoba N21098.*

Although Labour MLA Fred Dixon was not a member of the Strike Committee, he supported its demands. On May 23, he was interviewed by Johnson.

I had a chat with him yesterday, and his opinion emphatically was that the workers were not weakening and were as determined as ever to secure collective bargaining and to get an official guarantee of it. Mr. Dixon also defended the whole idea of sympathetic strikes. "The whole working class," he said. "feels that in the past it has suffered and conditions have been against it…Labor never has recognized so keenly the essential need of solidarity, and this, they say, they will maintain at all costs." Mr. Dixon, in answer to a question, laughed at the idea that an attempt had been made to set up Soviet rule. There had been negotiations constantly between the Strike Committee and the city authorities. "Did that look like usurpation?" he asked.

CHAPTER 2

ENTER THE SOLDIERS

MAY 24–28

On May 24, the *Winnipeg Tribune* and *Winnipeg Telegram* resumed publication with limited editions. Meighen and Robertson met with Mayor Gray, Citizens members and various officials. Robertson told Strike Committee representatives he would make no effort to settle the dispute until all public services were restored. *Tribune* reporter Arthur Caylor visited the Citizens and Strike Committee headquarters. On May 25, the first Labor Church service was held in Victoria Park in front of five thousand people. The same day, Robertson met with seventy-five striking postal employees at the city's main post office.

On May 26, City Council passed resolutions firing all civic employees who had joined the strike, preventing Winnipeg firemen from joining international unions and obliging candidates for the fire brigade to promise not to join any future sympathy strikes. Alfred Andrews was appointed special representative of the Justice Department in Winnipeg by Arthur Meighen. The provincially operated telephone system and the post office were partially functioning again with replacement workers. However, only sixteen out of three hundred postal workers returned to work, and streetcar service had still not resumed. Arthur Meighen left Winnipeg for Ottawa.

A heat wave that had begun in Winnipeg on May 21 peaked on May 28 at ninety-five degrees Fahrenheit.

The *Winnipeg Tribune* resumed publication on May 24. In this issue, the paper's editor, John J. Moncrieff, wrote "Violation of the Great Fundamental Principles of Constitutional Government" to identify those who caused the walkout and indicate their "design."

> *In the present instance the violators are composed of a comparatively small coterie of agitators with Bolshevik tendencies and Bolshevik methods who have seized upon the stressful times and the reconstruction days in our history to trample in the dust, to the full extent of their ingenuity and powers, the laws, the ideals, and the civilization of our day...The design—the real design of the "soviet"—to set up a revolutionary government has miserably failed. The plot is revealed in all its hideousness.*

On the same day, the *Tribune* ran a story by reporter Arthur Caylor, the only Winnipeg newspaperman to be given a byline during the strike and one of the few to visit the Strike Committee and Citizens headquarters. In "All Aboard for Winnipeg's Two Strike 'Capitals,'" Caylor provided a "personally conducted" trip inside the Labor Temple (Strike Committee headquarters) and Trade Board Building (Citizens headquarters). He began at the Labor Temple.

> *You push your way through a dense knot of men grouped about the entrance, intent on roughly lettered bulletins. They are men who have lately doffed their overalls and put on their Sunday clothes. The strike is at once a holiday and a grave time to them. They haven't much to say. The watchword, they are told, is "Say nothing, do nothing, think nothing—just wait"...As you push up the long steps you find yourself gently oozed over to the right of a dividing rope line by a director of traffic. Suddenly the crush drops apart and you are in a long room, flanked on one side by a cigar counter, on the other by a rank of tiny offices partitioned off along the wall. Probably a hundred men are milling through the room. All are smoking. The air is thick and hot.*

Then he depicted the scene in the upper floors.

> *Many meetings are on in the various rooms, but by the time you reach the fourth floor you have reached more sacred precincts where fewer come and*

more is done. It is here that the strike committee is determining the policies that later will be denounced by its opponents as further attempts at soviet rule. You walk into a large ante-room. There are a few men scattered about. Someone rushes up to the guard at the door, who is listening intently, his ear at the peep-hole…A moment later the door opens. Out rushes a delegate. He is in a hurry to get back, for much is going on inside. Through the open door you see a mass of men and a few women. The room—a big one—is jammed. The air is blue with smoke. Some of the men are coatless.

Finally, he described a striker guarding the main meeting room of the Strike Committee.[10]

On your way out you pass a door. It opens on a carpetless [sic] office room. There are several desks and a telephone. A safe stands in one corner. If Brother Bricklayer Owen would let you pass you would find yourself right in the centre of things for it is here that the inner committee of 15 holds its sessions…But you will not get by while Brother Owen's good right arm holds out.

Next he described the Citizens headquarters.

But as you enter the low rambling building on your right, where the Citizens' committee of 1,000 holds its sessions, things are different. The Sunday suit of the striker has given way to the tailor's best. The powerful pipe has made room for the fragrant Havana [cigar]…However, although the crowd is smaller, there is no less activity. At the door you find a desk where you can sign up as a fireman or a telephone operator or join the militia or whatnot…Now and then a committee man comes down the steps. He attempts to hurry by without seeing anyone. But does he? He does not. He is stopped by Ed, the capitalist, or the Hon. Bill KC, or Joe the banker, who demands to know what is going on and what it is all about.

Caylor finished by contrasting each side's philosophy. "The great contrast between the two capitols, you will notice, is that at the labor temple the word is 'Do Nothing.' At the board of trade it is 'Do Something.' At the labor temple they are sitting tight waiting for something to turn up. At the board of trade they are organizing, planning, preparing for any eventuality."

On May 26, the *Toronto Telegram* ran Mary Snider's second dispatch "Lawyer Doffs His Gown, Office Man His Coat, to Fight Fires" in which she again praised the Citizens.

A million and a half dollars [sic] worth of motor cars belonging to business men are parked around the headquarters of the Citizens' Committee. They are at the city's service for police, fire, military, and other transportation work. They [volunteers] would probably run the streetcars if they didn't think it will give the strikers a taste of their own medicine…here business men toil ten, twelve and fifteen hours daily in an endeavor to protect homes and keep families of all citizens from suffering.

On the same day, the *Toronto Star* published dispatches from both Plewman and Johnson. In "Metal Workers' Strike Started the Trouble," Plewman reported the origin of the strike.

Just what did happen in Winnipeg? As nearly as the writer can determine, this is in brief what happened. Three weeks ago the Metal Trades workers in contract shops went on strike to enforce collective bargaining as they have it on the railways. The building trades also struck to enforce the same principle. Twelve days ago, the [Winnipeg] Trades and Labor Council, which within a year has unionized all the clerks, waiters, food makers and distributors, and movie employees, called a general sympathetic strike to assist the fight for collective bargaining.

Then he described reaction to this development.

The non-striking elements of the community at once envisioned Russian Bolshevism and organized military and other forces to secure the essentials of life. In the meantime, the strikers, who claim they had no intention other than to show their power to cut off supplies, arranged with the Mayor to partially operate some of the services and tack up words on bread and milk wagons, restaurants, and movies, indicating that the service was by permission of the strike committee. The entire community, barring strikers, was enraged by this development, which was interpreted as meaning that the employers were being given permission to do business. Instead of that the strikers were being allowed to serve the public.

In "Robertson and Meighen Declare No Justification for Walkout," Johnson commented on the belief by Meighen and Robertson that the strike was a revolutionary plot.

With the statements of Hon. Arthur Meighen and Senator Robertson, Minister of labor, to the effect that they regarded the Winnipeg general strike as a cloak for something deeper—a cloak for an effort to "overturn proper authority"—the question of whether or not the strike here really has had an ulterior motive in the form of a Soviet plot becomes a dominate issue again. It is well known, however, that members of the Provincial Government, like the Federal men, are convinced in their own minds that an unlawful and unconstitutional effort was made here to usurp power. It is the view firmly held also by thousands of citizens, although it is denied flatly by the strikers themselves and their leaders.

Next Johnson explained the importance of their interpretation.

Not only is the right or wrong of this matter of fundamental importance, but the mere fact that the "plot" idea is held, not only by private citizens, but by responsible Ministers of the Crown both Federally and Provincially, is a most important factor in the situation. Whether their view actually is well-founded or not, they believe it is, and their belief has led them to come out definitely against the strike. They are not preserving neutrality, they are openly opposed to it.

Finally, he suggested who was behind the strike.

When the smoke has cleared away, what may be discovered is this. A very large number of trade unionists, probably the vast majority struck on the simple and specific issue of collective bargaining, which they thought was being assailed in such a challenging way that there was no recourse but to clear the issue once for all. A small proportion of men probably did have some plan of taking over at least civic authority and of ruling Winnipeg under decentralized Soviet form with proletarian dictatorship. A larger proportion, although in all probability a distinct minority, if you actually count heads, had another vision which may well be the crux of the whole situation, as far as the "conspiracy" is concerned. What this last class of men wanted was not political control at all, but a direct step towards the control of industry by the workers themselves and towards the policy of production for use rather than for profit.

Also on May 26 the *Toronto Telegram* ran a dispatch from Porter. In "Revolution Their Chief Aim with 'Peg as Starting Point," he again praised the Citizens.

The Winnipeg situation offers the possibility of an object lesson for the benefit of all Canada in stamping out Bolshevism. That lesson is the proper and effective organization of the rest of the citizens through "citizens committees of one thousand" in every city throughout the Dominion. This organization of society against the Reds…is a sort of self defence league, which should be spread and branches formed throughout the country for the citizens' committee has performed a wonderful work here in these trying days for Winnipeg. The proposition should not stop here with the ending of the revolution…The citizens' committee of a thousand should not disband but should expand its organization until we have in effect a citizens' committee consisting of millions of people between coast and coast.

On the same day, in "Why Thousands of Men and Women Are on Strike in Winnipeg," the *Telegram*'s editor, Knox Magee, emphasized the revolutionary nature of the strike.

There are in Winnipeg unfortunately a handful of English and Scotch agitators who are openly and even proudly "Red" Socialists and anarchists. They are held in contempt by their own fellow countrymen and are despised and loathed by all decent men of any nationality and are admired and followed only by the hostile alien element…The working man's common sense has deserted him. That is the psychological moment for the quack, the Socialist, the anarchist, the Bolshevik with his general strike pain killer, his anti-capitalist, anti-toxin, his Soviet sleep producer…How many British subjects would be on strike to-day if before it came into effect they had realized it was not to be a strike but a treacherous attempt at revolution?

In "The People's Hope," Moncrieff reiterated the specter of Bolshevism. "It has been demonstrated beyond any question of doubt that the comparatively small lawless element, speaking in the name of Labor, that would introduce lawlessness into this part of Canada, has been shown that the citizens possess a general and physical power that will not tolerate Bolshevism."

Two days later, in a *Vancouver Sun* dispatch headlined "Winnipeg Workers Losing $150,000 a Day by Strike," Canadian Press Winnipeg bureau manager J.F.B. Livesay commented on the agency's telegraphers joining the strike.[11]

If the strikers' committee designed to strike a note of terrorism across the Dominion, their purpose was well served by permitting the free circulation of wild reports, while they prevented the fair and moderate statement of the facts by the Canadian Press Limited through calling out its telegraphers. If on the other hand their intent was to conduct an orderly demonstration of their strength along legitimate channels, then they were ill-advised to close down the local daily newspapers on the one hand and on the other to tie-up regular news service to outside points.

MAY 29–JUNE 2

On May 29, City Council announced a May 30 deadline for Winnipeg police to sign a loyalty pledge promising never again to strike before arbitration of any dispute with the city or participate in a sympathetic strike. In the evening, a three-hour meeting of returned soldiers sympathetic to the strike was chaired by A.E. Moore, ex-sergeant and member of the province's Alien Investigation Board. As a result of the meeting, a veterans' march was planned for May 31 to confront Premier Norris at the Manitoba legislature. General Ketchen urged Mayor Gray to employ a force of special police before attempting to reinstate streetcar service. The first in a series of full- and half-page anti-strike advertisements from the Citizens appeared in the *Winnipeg Telegram*. More than 230 members of the fire department rejected the city's new loyalty pledge. General Ketchen and Alfred Andrews informed Mayor Gray that the Royal North West Mounted Police (RNWMP) would not be used to replace city policemen if they walked off their jobs. Mail delivery was resumed in the downtown districts.

The May 30 deadline for police to sign the loyalty pledge was extended to June 3. The *Citizen* published the first in a series of full-page anti-strike ads. The next day, about twelve thousand pro-strike returned soldiers marched on the Manitoba legislature. Led by Moore and returned soldier Roger Bray, about two thousand men confronted Premier Norris in the legislature's main chamber. The ex-servicemen then marched to City Hall to confront Mayor Gray. A railway men's mediation board was established to examine the issue of collective bargaining (union recognition) in the strike. Also on May 31, *Chicago Tribune* reporter Arthur Maybury Evans arrived in Winnipeg, and the first Citizens anti-strike advertisement appeared in the *Free Press* and *Tribune*.[12]

On June 1, Gideon Robertson left Winnipeg for Ottawa. During the day, members of the Winnipeg Police Commission, Citizens members, Premier

Don't Be Misled—The Only Issue Is Bolshevism

Citizens, including workers, should no longer permit themselves to be misled by the Bolshevist leaders, who through their newspaper mouthpiece, in large type every day, state that the issues of the so-called strike are:

1. The Right to Collective Bargaining.

2. A Living Wage.

The Western Labor News strike bulletin says "There are no other issues."

The statements of the strike bulletin as to the issues are entirely misleading and deceptive.

As shown elsewhere in this issue, the right to collective bargaining has never been challenged by any employer involved in the original dispute upon which this so-called general strike was called.

No employer in the City of Winnipeg challenges or denies the right of the workers to bargain collectively.

Every employer wants all his employes to not only have "A Living Wage," but more than a living wage.

No employer in the City of Winnipeg strike, or revolution, has refused to recognize collective bargaining.

No employer involved in the Winnipeg strike, or revolution, has refused the workers a living wage.

To state otherwise is grossly to pervert the truth.

There is only ONE ISSUE before the public for decision at the present time : THE RIGHT OF THE PEOPLE TO LIVE THEIR OWN LIVES, TO CARRY ON THEIR NORMAL ACTIVITIES, TO HAVE POLICE AND FIRE PROTECTION AND ADEQUATE FOOD AND WATER, without having to ask the permission of a Strike Committee, or Soviet.

The issue is to decide whether or not any section of the community may deliberately throttle the whole community, for any purpose or at any time.

The issue is Bolshevism versus Constitutional Government.

The issue is the principle of the General Strike as a weapon for enabling a Bolshevist few to ride roughshod over the citizens at large.

And if we submit to it now, we shall have to submit to it again and again, just whenever any few workers and their employers cannot agree, or after agreeing, fall out again.

Who, in Winnipeg, wants to face a repetition of the General Strike—or Revolution ? Don't be misled—KILL IT NOW.

Advertisement in *Winnipeg Citizen*, May 30.

Opposite: Citizens advertisement in *Winnipeg Tribune*, May 31.

Norris, Attorney General Johnson and the editors of the *Free Press*, *Telegram* and *Tribune* met at Mayor Gray's residence to discuss the imposition of the police loyalty oath. On June 2, another pro-strike march on the legislature of between seven and nine thousand returned men was organized. The next day, pro-strike veteran Roger Bray led a third parade to the legislature and then to Citizens headquarters at the Board of Trade offices in the Industrial Bureau.

On May 29, the *Toronto Telegram* published two stories by Snider. In "Filth Festered Under Gospel of 'Do Nothing,'" she once more applauded the Citizens.[13] "But nothing daunts the Citizens' Committee. All business men have abandoned their own interests, and work together for the city's welfare. Their personal affairs are neglected. Never did one big community [a reference to the One Big Union] pull with such ardor and unanimity. While strikers 'do nothing,' they [volunteers] are prepared to do everything."[14]

In "Dictator of Do-Nothing Dangles Hope Before Dupes," she described Ivens after listening to him address a Sunday night open-air service at Victoria Park.

> *It is easy to see why his opponents say he is clever but dangerous. He is sincere. He means what he said when urging strikers to "keep quiet" but in the same breath he scattered anger embers by asserting he could give the name of the man, the number of his auto, and the names of the men in the car with him who that very day boasted they would "send out of Winnipeg for gunmen and get Ivens." Such a statement is absolutely out of tune with public sentiment.*

On the same day, Ivens published "A Fine Chorus" to express the strikers' frustration over lack of progress in settling the walkout.

> *Senator Robertson:—I can do nothing till the posties return to work.*
> *Premier Norris:—I can do nothing till you call off the sympathetic strike.*
> *City Council:—We can do nothing till the civic employees return.*
> *Board of Trade:—We can do nothing till you all go back.*
> *The Strikers:—(Discordant Voice) We can do nothing till you all come forward.*

The next day, the *Montreal Star* published dispatches by Porter and Conklin. Porter described the Citizens' intent to inform Canadians and Americans of the Bolshevist nature of the strike.

> *There is no spirit of compromise on the part of the business interests. On the contrary each passing hour finds the members of the committee of one thousand strengthening its position, getting the situation more in hand, better prepared to carry on to the end…To the end that the people of Canada and the United States may know what the situation is here*

and the exact threat it conveys to the rest of this country, the Committee of One Thousand is preparing a brief, covering a history of the strike to date, the efforts of the citizens to oppose it, and defining the situation just as the committee sees it. In this brief the committee unceasingly calls the strike an outgrowth of Bolshevism.

Conklin reported on striker resolve.

The fight in Winnipeg following the general strike has settled down to a stiff proposition with no rift in the lute. All reports to contrary, there are no serious breaks in the union ranks, and where there are, many suspect the strikers are going back only to win the object of inducing those at work to leave. There is no compromise suggested now. As long as the Strike Committee are getting the support of the unions in other cities in Canada, and as long as there are unions ready to add to the numbers of those now idle, common ground will be difficult to reach.

On the same day, Ivens used the front page of *Western Labor News* to reinforce the strikers' demands.

What We Want

The Demands of the Strikers are:—
The Right of Collective Bargaining.
A Living Wage.
Reinstatement of all Strikers.

What We Do Not Want

Revolution.
Dictatorship.
Disorder.

The *Citizen*'s editor countered with "Don't Be Misled—The Only Issue Is Bolshevism," the first in a series of full-page anti-strike advertisements similar to those published at no charge by the *Free Press*, *Tribune* and *Telegram*.

Citizens, including workers should no longer permit themselves to be misled by the Bolshevist leaders, who through their newspaper mouthpiece, in large type every day, state that the issues of the strike are 1. The Right to Collective Bargaining 2. A Living Wage…The issue is to decide whether or not any section of the community may deliberately throttle the whole community, for any purpose at any time. The issue is Bolshevism versus Constitutional Government…Who, in Winnipeg, wants to face a repetition of the General Strike—or Revolution. Don't be misled. KILL IT NOW.

Meanwhile, in "A Hun-Like Diminuendo," Magee again conflated the strike with the Russian Revolution.

Today the conspirators fear to admit to those very men and women they have deceived and imposed upon—the men and women whom they have induced by false pretenses to a strike—that their object was and is revolution, the establishing of a Soviet form of Government after our honest British system should be overthrown—the erection in this City first and in Canada after, of Lenine's regime, with all its disgusting depravity, all its riot of loot, lewdness and lust; all its tyrannical oppression, bloodshed and famine.

Between May 30 and June 2, several thousand pro-strike veterans participated in a series of marches to the Manitoba legislature to force a settlement of the strike by Premier Norris. On May 30, Plewman accompanied the men who burst into the legislature's main chamber. His report of the exchange between veterans' spokesman Jack Moore and Premier Norris ran in the *Star* under the headline "Veterans Stand for Constituted Law, Authority."

At noon yesterday…two thousand veterans under the leadership of Jack Moore marched into the Parliament Buildings and occupied the Legislative chamber…Bedlam prevailed until the Premier appeared and sat down at the table below the dais…"I want you boys in the galleries to behave while I am speaking and the Premier is replying," said Moore…The veterans' spokesman pointed out that they had offered their lives for their country and were ready to protect the State and constituted authority. "I suppose no one has the guts to say we are Bolsheviki," he observed, and his comrades thundered their approval. "The Citizens' Committee has been talking about English and Scotch anarchists, and they've got to be stopped, and you can do it, Mr. Premier. All we want is living conditions. Some of our comrades are working 74 hours a week for $50 and $55 a month." "Shame!" "Disgrace!" shouted the galleries, and someone mentioned the *name of a newspaper as the offender. "We want collective bargaining as they have it on railways," continued Jack Moore. "I have had experience in labor negotiations and know that there can be no objection to collective bargaining in metal trade contract shops. That is all we want. The strike can be settled at once on that basis. It has gone on long enough and it's up to the Government to take a hand to bring the parties together and force a settlement." Premier Norris replied that his Government realized the importance of the question and needed no assurances that the veterans were not untrue to the State. He said the Government was doing all it could to bring about a settlement, but there was a difference of opinion as to what was collective bargaining, and offhand he could not venture definition…He thanked them for the trouble they had gone to in making their views known.*

Snider also covered veterans' parades. In "Veterans Counter Soldier Demonstration," she reported a June 2 counterdemonstration by anti-strike ex-servicemen. She quoted two of the returned men who participated in the march. "I don't believe any of our lads were in those [pro-strike] parades, and we have 1,400 men who have been overseas," said an official of the Imperial Veterans. "Those fellows who marched were mostly drafters, who were jerked away from here by the hair," said another veteran authority.

Meanwhile, Conklin and Porter continued their freelance reporting. On June 2, the *Halifax Herald* headlined Conklin's story "35,000 Winnipeg Strikers Who Have Remained Steadfast," in which he complimented the strikers and again dispelled the rumor that its leaders were foreigners.

Whether one is with the strikers or merely an observing neutral, with a tendency to favor the employers one must admire the loyalty of 35,000 strikers in Winnipeg who have through temptation and trial, remained steadfast in what they deem principle…A British flag of large proportions has always spread itself to the breeze from the top of the labor temple. All [strike] leaders are English or Scotch, although the aim of certain people has been to fasten the Jewish nationality on two of them…William Ivens, Methodist minister, who has been blamed for much of the Bolshevism stigma attached to the general strike, was born at Barford, Warwickshire, England.

The next day, the *Ottawa Journal* and *Halifax Chronicle* carried Conklin's dispatches. In the *Journal*, his story reported, "There is no danger that the [pro-strike] returned men and strikers are getting into an ugly temper," and in his account in the *Chronicle*, he described a march by pro-strike veterans

WINNIPEG'S GENERAL STRIKE

to City Hall and the Industrial Bureau and quoted them as shouting, "We are the citizens, not the Citizens' Committee. We'll show the Citizens' Committee who are the citizens. We fought for a dollar ten a day, now we want a living wage."

On June 2, Porter supplied the *Toronto Telegram* with an interview he had conducted with Gideon Robertson. The paper headlined the story "'One Big Union' Faces Defeat: Sane Labor Men See Its Folly."

> *Before leaving for the east yesterday* [June 1], *the Minister of Labor, Senator Gideon Robertson, after being here for ten days taking an active part in the efforts to settle the general strike, gave the writer an interview in which he very definitely stated the position of the Government. The minister said: "The promoters of the general strike in Winnipeg now sit in the ashes of their folly…Labor leaders who advocate that might is right, who hold that law, justice and honor should be discarded at will, merit and receive the condemnation of good citizens. In a general sympathetic the force is directed against the whole community who are innocent of any responsibility for the offence…Therefore sympathetic strikes must always fail.*

On the same day, the *Chicago Tribune* ran the first dispatch by reporter Arthur Evans, who had just arrived in Winnipeg.[15] The American daily headlined his story "Social Revolt Is Purpose of Canada Strike."

> *Canada's spreading general strike, from all indications, is a pure and simple effort to overthrow the present industrial system. It has all the aspects of the Seattle strike engineered by the I.W.W. minus the violence. The Winnipeg tie-up is only the nucleus. At the foundation is the "one big union" idea, which is merely another name for the type of industrial organization urged by the I.W.W. Its goal is "proletarian dictatorship" which is what Russia is getting from the Bolshevists…These are not chance observations for one finds these ideas exploited in the literature of the Canadian strike movement…The extremists have climbed into the saddle. In Winnipeg one finds leaders of all grades from the cautious to the fanatical.*

Also on June 2, the *Toronto Globe* headlined a report from Evans "On Brink of Martial Law," in which he commented on Winnipeg's returned soldiers.

> *One surprising feature to the outsiders is the part the returned soldiers are taking in the general strike which has for background the One Big Union*

idea, which is a plain unadulterated Soviet Government, such as Russia's experiencing. A canvass by secret agents of the Government, it is said, shows that only about 10 per cent of the returned soldiers are participating in the strike…The great bulk of the soldiers are strikers too, the agents declare, and are men who were caught by conscription late in the war, and did not see actual service on the battlefield.

Another view of returned soldiers was provided by Samuel Hopkins.

Both sides are bidding for him. Both sides are vehemently denouncing him when he disappoints them. Both sides are employing every appeal to factionalism, prejudice, and self-interest in his mind for, however solemnly they may deny it, both sides are basing hopes upon him as the determinant of victory…His state of mind is peculiar and complicated. He has come home, an acclaimed hero, only to find living conditions harsher than when he went away, prices higher, few jobs open to him at the improved wages which he needs in order to meet new conditions, and in many cases his place filled by an alien who is not only an alien but an enemy alien, Austrian or German. For this he blames the Government…He is universally "sore," often even revolutionary in spirit. He does not approve of Bolshevism. And he wants labor to "show him" that its present uprising will fulfill his desires without disrupting and dissolving orderly government.

CHAPTER 3

WHO OWNS THE STREETS?

JUNE 3-8

On June 3, well-known American photojournalist James Hare of *Leslie's Weekly* magazine began a three-day assignment in Winnipeg to photograph the strike.[16] On June 4, the Strike Committee again stopped deliveries of milk, bread and ice, and in response, dairy owners and city officials set up emergency distribution depots at several Winnipeg schools. The *Free Press* printed a front-page notice inviting all anti-strike veterans to meet at Broadway Avenue and Main Street at 11:00 a.m. On the same day, parades by returned soldiers for and against the strike almost clashed in front of the Manitoba legislature. Anti-strike banners declared, "We Will Maintain Constituted Authority, Law & Order, to Hell with the Alien Enemy" and "God Save the King." Pro-strike banners proclaimed, "We Stand For 35,000 Against 1,000,"[17] "We Fought the Hun Over There. We Fight the Hun Everywhere" and "Deport All Undesirables."

On June 5, Major Hilliard Lyle was appointed to organize special police, and Captain J. Dunwoody was placed in charge of mounted men. Andrews arranged a meeting with Premier Norris, Attorney General Johnson, General Ketchen, RNWMP representatives, Mayor Gray and Alderman Fowler to discuss arresting the strike leadership. In the afternoon, a confrontation occurred

Citizens volunteers line up on Broadway Avenue, June 5. *Courtesy of Archives of Manitoba N12304, Winnipeg Strike 13.*

Norris addressing anti-strike Loyalist veterans, June 4. Note the reporter in front of Gray writing on a notepad. *Courtesy of Archives of Manitoba N12297, Winnipeg Strike 6.*

Anti-strike Loyalists veterans prepare to march on June 4. *Courtesy of Archives of Manitoba N12295, Winnipeg Strike 4.*

Anti-strike Loyalists veterans' demonstration at City Hall, June 4. *Courtesy of Archives of Manitoba N2737, Foote 1671.*

in front of City Hall between returned soldiers of opposing parades. A tentative plan for settlement of the strike was presented by the Running Trades Mediation Committee, and Mayor Gray issued his first proclamation prohibiting marches and assemblies of crowds on city streets.

> *By the authority vested in me, I do hereby order that all persons do refrain from forming or taking part in any parades or congregating in crowds or upon the streets of the City of Winnipeg, and do hereby request of all law-abiding citizens the full compliance with this proclamation.*

On June 6, the Canadian government introduced amendments to the Immigration Act permitting deportation without trial of anyone not born in Canada who was accused of sedition. The *Act to Amend the Immigration Act*, which took only forty-five minutes to be given three readings in the House of Commons and Senate, was targeted against the British-born leaders of the Winnipeg strike. The following day, Mayor Gray addressed a large crowd of strikers and veterans at Victoria Park, which had been renamed Soldiers' Parliament, and several returned soldiers were signed as special constables. On June 8, former Winnipeg minister James S. Woodsworth arrived in Winnipeg and that evening spoke at the Sunday Labor Church service at Victoria Park to ten thousand people.

James Hare's photo story in *Leslie's*, titled "Canada's Fight Against Bolshevism," provided a gallery of twelve photographs. Two side-by-side pictures taken on June 3 showed a large crowd of pro-strike veterans assembled in front of the Industrial Bureau. The first photograph was captioned, "Strikers about to tear down sign from the Board of Trade doorway in the Industrial Building, Winnipeg 'Headquarters of Citizens' Committee of One Thousand.' Though small fights have occurred regularly, there has been no mob violence except in the matter of destroying signs, newspapers, etc." The second photograph was captioned, "The same doorway a few moments later after the sign was torn down. This demonstration followed a visit to the Parliament buildings to demand new legislation favorable to the strikers. The general strike began in May over a trivial labor dispute, but it developed into a matter of 'Bolsheviks' vs. 'bourgeois.'"

In contrast, three of Hare's photographs shot on June 4 featured anti-strike returned soldiers. One taken at the corner of Main Street and Broadway Avenue showed a parade of veterans and was captioned, "The Canadian general strike has settled down to the bitterest fight between union labor and

Pro-strike veterans at Citizens Headquarters in the Winnipeg Board of Trade building, June 3. Note the Citizens sign over the left entrance. *Courtesy of Archives of Manitoba N12298, Winnipeg Strike 7.*

The crowd has by now removed the Citizens sign, June 4. *Courtesy of Archives of Manitoba N12299, Winnipeg Strike 8.*

City clerk swearing in special police, June 5 or 6. *Courtesy of Archives of Manitoba N12307, Winnipeg Strike 16.*

a community that the western world has seen. Canada looks upon the strike as a finish fight against the soviet idea in government." A second featured the same veterans in front of City Hall with signs reading, "Down with Bolshevism, We Will Maintain Constituted Authority, Law & Order" and "Deport the Undesirable Alien." A third with Premier Norris addressing anti-strike servicemen near the legislature was captioned, "Premier Norris denounced the strikers' parade because of its leaders, who advocated Bolshevism. He refused to write his resignation or to promise new legislation unless the people of the province demanded it in a constitutional manner." Another photograph, taken on either June 5 or 6, featured Winnipeg's city clerk swearing in special police who were to replace the regular police force on June 9 and was captioned, "Swearing in special constables at the City Hall. Owing to the disaffection of the police and the firemen it was necessary to swear in great numbers of citizens as special officers. Enough of them are being sworn to give protection to all men desiring to return to work. The police department is undergoing reorganization."

On June 4, the Strike Committee again suspended the delivery of milk, bread and ice. The following day, the *Citizen*'s editor wrote "Child Murder Will Be Punished."

THE WINNIPEG CITIZEN

Vol. 1   June 5, 1919.   Published in Winnipeg in the interest of the Citizens.   No. 16

An Attempt at Wilful Murder

Read this extract from the report of the Food Committee of the Central Strike Committee, published in the Western Labor News Strike Bulletin No. 1 on May 18:

"After making a thorough investigation of the depot scheme we found it would be impossible to distinguish between the sick children, owing to the fact that it would take days to establish a card system and REPORTS WERE FAST COMING IN OF CHILDREN ON THE VERGE OF DEATH FOR THE WANT OF MILK. We then decided to open up the supply of milk through the regular method of supply."

Read that quotation again carefully and you cannot fail to realize that the action of the Strike Committee in again attempting to stop the delivery of milk is equivalent to an attempt at wilful murder.

The delivery of milk was cut off upon the day that the general strike was started. Within two days the strike committee had to resume the delivery of milk, because REPORTS WERE FAST COMING IN OF CHILDREN ON THE VERGE OF DEATH FOR THE WANT OF MILK.

In plain language, because their action was upon the point of killing babies, the regular delivery of milk was resumed.

The regular delivery of milk has continued since, up to 11 a.m. yesterday, solely because any interruption in that regular delivery would again bring "CHILDREN ON THE VERGE OF DEATH FOR THE WANT OF MILK."

Having delivered milk after the first two days of strike, to keep children from death for the want of milk, the Strike Committee has now ordered the delivery stopped, knowing full well that that stoppage is bound—if it is permitted—to starve babies to death.

Knowing that, and having admitted it in their first food committee report, it must be presumed that the Strike Committee, in again stopping the delivery of milk, intends that babies shall be starved to death for the want of milk.

So that the stoppage of the delivery of milk is absolutely equivalent to an attempt at wilful murder. The same remark applies so far as people other than children are concerned, to the stoppage of the delivery of bread.

This is a situation that calls for most drastic and firm action. If a man goes out to slug another to death with a lead pipe, and he is caught bringing the weapon down on the other fellow's head, he is arrested and charged with attempted murder.

If a clique of revolutionists conspire in the Labor Temple to starve babies to death for the want of milk, and then take the first essential step to accomplish that end, they apparently go scot-free.

It means that there is no law in Winnipeg. We have lots of talk from the Strike Committee about law and order, and while they talk their hypocrisy serves as a smoke-screen for the fact that we have neither law nor order.

Lawlessness and disorder are rampant throughout the city all day and every day. Men and women are wantonly assaulted upon the streets. Men, women and children are attacked and threatened while going about their lawful avocations.

Postmen carrying mail to strikers' houses are daily beaten. Yesterday a mob went to the house of one postman, damaged the fences, trampled the garden and terrorized the man's wife. They hanged the postman in effigy in his own backyard, making the man's wife believe that they were actually hanging her husband. She was frightened into unconsciousness and did not recover from the coma for two hours.

Every morning automobiles carrying workers to and from their places of employment are stoned, and nothing seems to be accomplished toward stopping it. Two women selling newspapers at the corner of Portage and Main last night at 6 o'clock were roughly assaulted.

Drivers of delivery-rigs are also daily assaulted and the most unseemly of disorderly demonstrations has taken place upon the streets. Yesterday a disorderly mob visited Fort Rouge and demonstrated against some of the big residences there.

The Crescent and other creamery concerns have been forced to throw thousands of gallons of milk into the sewers because they were not allowed either to distribute it, nor to make it up into by-products.

A city alderman, it is reported, went to a place where newsboys were delivering papers yesterday and threatened them; another individual appeared and used even stronger language, telling the boys they would be killed if they continued delivering newspapers.

Hoodlums daily create disorders on the streets, tearing up newspapers and insulting those who buy them, and assaulting boys whose business it is to distribute those papers to the homes. War on babies, women and children seems to be the principal weapon of the strike committee—and who with any sense will say that this sort of thing is designed to enforce "collective bargaining."

What power have the babies "on the verge of death for want of milk," to enforce collective bargaining? What power have the newsboys who deliver newspapers, to enforce collective bargaining? The whole thing is getting entirely beyond the stage where velvet gloves should be used in handling it.

It is time that all of the measures that are prescribed by the law of the land, should be put into effect to restore law and order in Winnipeg. If the restoration of law and order require the most drastic step that the law prescribes, then that step should and must be taken.

This Paper is Distributed Free — Don't Pay For It

Winnipeg Citizen front-page editorial, June 5.

At a public meeting of the Civic Committee on bread and milk supply yesterday, officials of the Central Strike Committee plainly stated that the Central Strike Committee had requested the dairymen and bread workers to again come out on strike. President James Winning, of the Trades and Labor Council, attempted to pass along the responsibility by stating that the Strike Committee could not "order" them, and that in going out again on strike the workers in question came out "voluntarily." The attempt to load the responsibility upon the workers themselves is more than interesting in view of the fact that R.B. Graham, crown prosecutor, has informed the Strike Committee, through the policemen's delegates to that body, that the moment one child dies in Winnipeg through being deprived of milk, the leaders of the Strike Committee will be charged with and placed on trial for murder.

Magee responded to the strikers' action with "Declare War on the Babies."

When the delivery of milk and bread was resumed after the first two days of the strike, the strike committee excused their action on the ground that it was necessary to do so because "reports were fast coming in of children on the verge of death for the want of milk." To avoid child murder, therefore, the strike committee allowed the resumption of delivery. To resume the former attitude of non-delivery, therefore, is knowingly to conspire to commit child-murder…By the decision to stop the deliveries of milk and bread, the strike leaders have declared war upon the babies.

On 7 June, despite the fact that Mayor Gray had made arrangements to deliver milk and bread to the citizens of Winnipeg, Dafoe wrote "Baby Killing." First he fixed responsibility for consequences on the Strike Committee.

The renewed interruption of the supply of milk and bread to the householders of Winnipeg brings uppermost the question of responsibility for the rise in the rate of infantile mortality which will inevitably accompany it. If the number of deaths among children through deprivation of the accustomed supply of milk increases—and that it will do so is a fact admitted by the strike committee as well as by the medical authorities—these additional deaths will lie at the door of the strike committee.

Then he compared the actions of the Strike Committee with those of the German High Command.

When the German High Command deliberately directed its Zeppelins to raid the open towns of Britain and France and caused the destruction by bombs of infants and school children, they drew upon themselves the contempt and opprobrium of civilized people everywhere. Between the German Zeppelin policy and that of cutting off the food of infants and children through the sympathetic strike there is no perceptible difference. The "baby-killers" of Europe hoped to do precisely what the strike committee in the city hopes to do—to bring the war to an end on their own terms by means of ruthlessness and frightfulness—of terrorism and oppression of the non-combatant population.

The ongoing parades and demonstrations by returned soldiers also resulted in considerable press reaction. Following the anti-strike veterans' June 4 march to confront Mayor Gray and Premier Norris, Snider wrote "'Down with Bolshevism!' Thunder 10,000 Soldiers." In this dispatch, she first quoted Gray.

"We all know that away behind the labor trouble is the Red Element sent here by other countries" said Mayor Gray addressing a crowd of eight or ten thousand, packed back of the City Hall at the Market Square this morning. He hoped "those fellows who are being misled would get some sense" and said if they did not "we will have to teach them." The soldiers addressed were ready to act as instructors instanter [sic]. Very wisely the strikers had been urged by their leaders to keep inside their homes today…Mr. Bray, the striking soldiers' representative, had said: "he told me [Norris] he was a soviet man and in favor of soviet government." "There is a vicious attempt to overthrow constituted authority, but that band of soviets will never get the ascendancy if you gentlemen stand behind us." "Put them in jail." "We will be behind you" "Call out the firing squad," yelled the crowd…Three Canadian flags and a Union Jack were carried, with banners reading: "Canadian Corps Fall In" "Deport the Undesirable Alien" "Down with Bolshevism" "To Hell with the Enemy Alien, God Save the King."

After June 4, veterans became involved in increasingly violent acts. One such incident was reported by Porter on June 5 in the *Toronto Telegram* under the headline "Austrian in 'Peg Beat Up." His account reflected the strong anti-alien sentiment of many ex-servicemen.

There was but one recorded incident yesterday of flag snatching. The victim was Capt. C.F.G. Wheeler vice-president of the Imperial war Veterans. At least Wheeler was to have been the victim, but a six foot Austrian ultimately proved to be the man that the ambulance carried from the scene. Wheeler is rather a quiet looking chap, he hails from the county of Down and has a good natured smile that apparently deceived the alien. In addition, Wheeler has a discharge paper that shows he has served only forty-four years in the British service, and some medals he added to his string at the Dardenelles [sic] and other bloody battle scenes in the war. The Irish veteran was proceeding in a casual way up Main Street, with a bit of an old Union Jack draped on his coat lapel. The Austrian, with an oath in the tongue of his fatherland, reached for it. The oath was the last word he uttered for the next half hour. He must have thought a concealed battery was sprung on him. Wheeler gave him a short arm jab, then he uppercut him twice, and as he was falling he got a half Nelson on the dazed Austrian and delivered a few more love taps. Then he dropped the remains on the sidewalk and a number of alien enemies who had stood back to watch their friend snatch Wheeler's flag picked up the Austrian wreck and the ambulance was called. Wheeler lit another cigarette and sauntered on up to [sic] Parliament Buildings to deliver an address to the returned soldiers an hour later.

On the same day, Plewman reported a confrontation between pro- and anti-strike returned men. His account appeared on June 6 under the headline "Many Free Fights Follow Parades of Rival Forces."

Black eyes are numerous in Winnipeg as the result of the free for all fighting at the corner of William and Main Streets in front of City Hall yesterday. Starting with the arrival of two parades at the City Hall, one in front and one in the rear, about noon yesterday long pent-up feelings of strikers and "antis" broke loose…As both parades dispersed at 12:30 each side got mixed up around the front of the hall. Some hotheads got into discussion, and then into punching heads. Police patrols and squads of police were soon dashing here and there into the crowds, making numerous arrests. They showed no discrimination…When the police had carried off the arrested men, the crowd thronged over Main Street, gathering in groups from sidewalk to sidewalk excitedly discussing what had happened. A part of the anti-strike parade started down Main Street towards James Street, and it was supposed they were about to raid the Labor Temple. Wiser councils prevailed.

Returned men were also mentioned in the June 6 editorial "A Safer City" by Moncrieff. "The swearing in of a large staff of special officers of the law was a step in the right direction…It is a gratifying fact, also, that the men sworn afresh to defend Canadian citizens, institutions and the honor of the nation's flag are, in the majority, if not possibly all men who defended Canadian and Empire honor at the front. Our homes are in safe keeping when the sworn guardians are our Returned Soldiers."

Meanwhile, Ivens used a front-page notice to caution pro-strike workers and returned soldiers.

Strikers, Hold Your Horses!
This is the hour when you can win
Steady, Boys Steady
Keep Quiet
Do Nothing
Keep Out Of Trouble
Leave this to your Enemies
Continue to prove that you are the friends of law and order

JUNE 9-16

On June 9, all but sixteen members of the Winnipeg police force were fired for refusing to sign the city's loyalty pledge. Hundreds of special police were then recruited by the city and paid six dollars per day, twice the temporary discharge allowance given to veterans. The next day, Chief Donald MacPherson was replaced by Deputy Chief Chris Newton as commander of the Winnipeg police force. Also on June 10, mounted special police armed with clubs clashed with pro-strike veterans, strikers and onlookers at the intersection of Portage Avenue and Main Street. During the confrontation, several hundred special police joined the fracas. On the same day, Gideon Robertson, along with South Winnipeg MP George Allan, returned to Winnipeg from Ottawa.[18]

On June 11, Mayor Gray issued a second proclamation banning public demonstrations. The tone was much stronger than his previous announcement and also warned of martial law.

To the Citizens of Winnipeg

If the hundreds of sightseers had not congregated on the main thoroughfare yesterday the disturbances would have been considerably curtailed. I urge all loyal citizens to go about their business and keep off the streets. Large crowds encourage lawlessness and hamper the police. In the interests of your city keep off the streets and avoid crowds. I wish to avoid the use of sterner methods if possible, but will use whatever methods are necessary to enforce law and order.

Also on June 11 the *Labor News* carried a front-page report that a CPR freight car loaded with machine guns had reached Winnipeg at 9:00 p.m. on June 10. On June 12, all commercial, brokerage and Canadian Press news agency telegraphers returned to their keys. William Pritchard, head of the Vancouver Longshoremen's Union, arrived in Winnipeg and, with returned soldier Roger Bray, James Woodsworth and Labour MLA Fred Dixon, addressed a crowd at Victoria Park.

On June 13 and 14, Winnipeg railway yard switchmen, firemen and enginemen began joining the strike. Robertson wired Prime Minister Borden that steps must be taken in Winnipeg to arrest strike leaders. The *Minneapolis Morning Tribune* reported that a twelve-man armoured machine gun tank was shipped into Winnipeg on the morning of June 12. On June 16, the metal shop employers published conciliatory proposals to meet metal trades workers' demands and prevented a strike by railway workers.

Snider visited Victoria Park on June 7 to listen to Mayor Gray and Roger Bray address a large crowd. Gray was there to explain the reasons for his June 5 proclamation banning parades; Bray, who by this point in the walkout had developed into an unofficial spokesman for the anti-strike veterans, followed Gray. On June 9, the *Toronto Telegram* published Snider's description of both men.

Coatless, pale-faced, receding chinned, leather belted, frail looking with baggy grey trousers, unpolished boots and droopy dark moustache, Bray, who is avowedly a Soviet advocate, looks the fanatic he is much more than the soldier he has been…[Gray] was alone in a largely hostile company, this young man of 35 or so, the wind lifting his slightly thinning fair hair and carrying clearly to the crowd every syllable he uttered. Brave men love bravery.

Roger Bray speaking at Victoria Park, June 13. *Courtesy of Archives of Manitoba N2742, Foote 1676.*

On the same day, several Canadian papers ran dispatches from Porter on the alleged presence of American secret service men in Winnipeg who were investigating Bolshevik money sent to strike leaders. The *Vancouver Sun* headlined Porter's story "Negotiations of Railway Brotherhood in Winnipeg to Settle Strike Fail."

> *United States secret service men in large numbers have arrived here* [Winnipeg] *investigating the alleged connection of strike leaders with agitators on the other side of the line. They claim to have evidence that some I.W.W. and Russian agitators they want in connection with recent bomb outrages in the States are concealed in Winnipeg. Especially are they trying to trace money sent from Chicago and New York into Winnipeg. One of these secret service men admitted today that they had direct evidence, names, dates and everything concerning one package of ten thousand dollars sent by revolutionary agents at Chicago to alleged soviet leaders in Winnipeg.*

On June 10, Snider wrote her last dispatch before leaving Winnipeg. In "Workers Want to Return," she again praised the Citizens. "The asphalt pavement outside the Industrial Bureau is worn in deep ruts by the kerb where cars come and go unceaselessly [*sic*]. The Committee of 1,000 are there till nearly midnight Sunday and every day...They are working now for the good of the city that prospered them as they worked for their own progress." Interestingly, the *Telegram* accompanied her report with a five-column photo of Gray addressing a crowd of returned soldiers at City Hall. The photo's title was "Down with Bolshevism: Deport Undesirables," and the caption read, "Returned soldiers assembly for an anti-strike demonstration back of the Winnipeg City Hall."

On the same day, the *Free Press* published "The Common Sense Approach," in which Dafoe appealed to the Strike Committee to call off the strike.

> *The middle of the fourth week of the strike finds this community more determined than ever to withstand the assault upon its rights. The endeavor of a small, but influential, section of the organized workers to enforce any of the demands which they may see fit to make, by holding the whole community ransom, has failed. The next move is with the strike committee...This is the common sense course for the strike committee, in its own interest and in the interest of those for whom it assumes to speak...It must recall its cry of "Stand and Deliver." It must admit that the sympathetic strike is not the weapon that it thought it was...All this must be done eventually. The part of wisdom is to accept the inevitable and do it now. But the initiative lies in this respect with the committee.*

Following the dismissal of all but a handful of Winnipeg's regular police force on June 9, hundreds of special constables were recruited to ensure law and order in Winnipeg. The next day, a confrontation occurred between mounted, baton-wielding specials and pro-labour veterans, strikers and bystanders at the intersection of Main Street and Portage Avenue. During the fighting, one of the mounted specials, decorated ex-sergeant major Frederick Coppins, disregarded orders from the troop's commanding officer not to move into the crowds on the sidewalk. As a result, thirty-year-old Coppins was injured and taken to Tuxedo Military Hospital, where more than two hundred veterans were convalescing from war wounds.

The next day, Plewman's account of the clash ran in both the *Toronto Star* and *Ottawa Journal*. The *Star* headlined his dispatch "100 with 'Broken' Heads in Winnipeg Disorders."

Crowd on Main Street at about 2:30 p.m., June 10. *Courtesy of Archives of Manitoba N12313, Winnipeg Strike 25.*

Mounted special police at Main Street and Portage Avenue at about 2:45 p.m., June 10. *Courtesy of Archives of Manitoba N12309, Winnipeg Strike 19.*

Mounted special police charging into the crowd on Main Street at about 3:00 p.m., June 10. *Courtesy of Archives of Manitoba N2741, Foote 1675.*

Baton-wielding special police marching east on Portage Avenue between 4:00 p.m. and 5:00 p.m., June 10. *Courtesy of Archives of Manitoba N12335, Winnipeg Strike 61.*

Sergt. Fred Coppins V.C., of the 8th Battalion, who went through the war without a scratch, was among the twenty "mounties" (special mounted police in mufti) who were injured in the battle with riotous strikers and strike sympathizers yesterday afternoon…The authorities say a hundred rioters are nursing "broken" heads at home. Five men in the mob were taken to one station. Excitement was tense for two hours [and it] *had looked as if the crowd would prove too much for the riders, when on orders from the Mayor they were withdrawn from the street at 5 o'clock and then the crowd quieted down. During the afternoon stones, rocks, eggs taken out of cafes, clubs dropped by the police in the melee were thrown at the horsemen from all directions…Mayor Gray is issuing a message to citizens warning them not to congregate as sterner measures will be used if necessary to prevent a repetition of the disturbances. Several individuals and at least one delegation saw Mayor Gray last night demanding martial law.*

Plewman's *Ottawa Journal* story provided additional details.

In one surge [by the mounted specials], *a woman with a baby carriage was caught. The perambulator was crushed to pieces but the babe was rescued. Mounties dashed pell mell down the sidewalks, wielding their clubs furiously and when they passed a woman lay on the sidewalk… Thirty Mounties would dash down the center of the road* [Main Street] *towards City Hall then wheel and return to Portage and Main, there to be "booed" and cheered and attacked. Sometimes they would charge in line two deep, stretching right across the road and sweeping all before them.*

Samuel Hopkins also provided a description of the event, as well as his opinion on its seriousness.

An amateur force was organized, drawn mainly from the ranks of returned soldiers. Armed with a clumsy sort of half club, half stave, they were sent out on horseback to clear the business section. The strikers were waiting for them. At the corner of the two main business streets the soldier-police were mobbed, and there followed what the papers described as the "worst riot in the history of Winnipeg." Apparently, the Canadian taste in riots is milder than ours. A running fight of fifteen minutes duration in the heart of the city between the police and a mob, in which not a shot is fired, not a man is killed, and hardly a window is broken, would scarcely be called a very serious riot in the United States. I hardly know what it would be called; a movie rehearsal, perhaps.

Evans's account of the confrontation appeared in the *Chicago Tribune* on June 11 under the headline "Strikers Battle Police."

Riot and violence tore loose on the streets of Winnipeg today. For three hours the strikers fought a pitched battle with the special constabulary in the heart of the city. Sergt. Frederick George Coppins, winner of the Victoria Cross in the great war, one of the special mounted constables was pulled from his horse and so maltreated he may die. Besides having two ribs broken from kicks and serious injuries to his head, Coppins suffered internal injuries.

The fracas also triggered editorial reaction. On June 11, Moncrieff published "Tuesday's Riot—The Mayor's Duty."

On Tuesday afternoon Civic Authority was set at defiance publicly on the most public corner and in the very heart of the city and under the very eye of—we are told—the Mayor himself, and yet there was lacking the assertion of the might of Canadian law...The man or any riotous body of men laying hands on, or assaulting one officer of the law, challenge the whole might of the law, Civic Provincial and Dominion. The duty of the Mayor and his associates was plain... That action was the reading of the Riot Act, thus placing the city under the protection of military law.

The *Citizen's* editor penned "Riot Born of Revolution."

At the time of writing, Sergeant Fred Coppins, Victoria Cross hero of France, is lying in the Military Hospital and is stated to be dying. He was not expected to live until morning. Sergeant Coppins swears that his injuries were caused by three Austrians who kicked him in front of Alloway and Champion's offices on Main street during the riot. By the time that this appears, Coppins may be dead. Whether he is dead or alive; whether he lives or dies, the fact remains that he was kicked with intent to kill, by three Austrians—men whose blood relatives he and every other returned fighter fought in France...This IS revolution with a vengeance.

This Strike Is More Dangerous to Winnipeg and Canada Than the War!

Do you realize this, Citizens of Winnipeg?

Do you realize that you, your family, your friends were condemned to starvation by the strike committee?

No milk, no bread, no water, no food—that was the program that the sympathetic strike meant.

We are not deprived altogether of these necessities of life and safety today; but if the strike committee had prevailed in its plan we would be without them!

Either that, or living under the authority and direction of Soviet government.

Don't consider the strike situation as it stands — consider it as the strike committee would have it stand.

These Men Were On Duty to Protect YOU and YOURS

Sergeant Coppin, V.C.

At Tuxedo Hospital

Reports this morning from the hospital are that Sergeant Coppin, who won the V.C. against the Huns over there, and nearly lost it in the struggle against the Huns in Winnipeg, is getting along as well as can be expected. The sergeant states he believes he can recognize the three alien enemies who attacked him.

Is This Law and Order?

The four special constables who were assaulted in a crowd of over one hundred strikers last night at Main and Higgins avenue, were all badly beaten up.

Thomas Sandall Morrison, who was shot and battered unconscious, was progressing favorably at the General hospital this morning.

Winnipeg Citizens!

Stay off the streets, away from crowds, and keep your women folk at home. You are creating trouble in congregating in crowds.

There Must Be Something Back of All This!

Something revolutionary that would cause the shrewd and callous leaders of the strike to take such drastic actions.

HERE'S THE REASON WHY:

Not wages, not hours, not unions, but "the one big opportunity to cause social revolution in Canada" was the reason back of this strike.

To pit brother workmen against brother workmen—to cause such unrest that no one could fathom the real cause—to upset living conditions so everyone would be dissatisfied, and then to pin the whole blame on those who are truly and sincerely working for the good of the whole citizenship, is the object of the strike leaders.

All this underlies the real reason which they never lose sight of — the destruction of our social fabric—the ushering in of the era of chaos known as Bolshevism.

Talk of playing with fire! Today Winnipeg and Canada are resting on a volcano which may erupt the boiling lava of horrible destruction, and only the actions of sane Canadianism are holding down the safety valve.

CITIZENS' COMMITTEE OF ONE THOUSAND

Citizens advertisement in *Winnipeg Telegram*, June 12.

Magee responded with "Weighed in the Balance."

Yesterday the badly adjusted mask [of the Red Five of Winnipeg] *was dropped and the grinning death's head was revealed. Its features are of the composite kind, in which the hideous visage of the Hun gorilla blends with that of the inhuman Bolshevik. Frankenstein's soulless monster was an angel of light compared with the Moloch to which the Red Five would have the citizens of Winnipeg pay homage, to which they would sacrifice the bound Canadian virgin and the helpless infant.*

In "Fine Business This!" Dafoe blamed Coppins's injuries on enemy aliens.

Young Winnipeg soldiers, returned men from years of overseas service, bearing with them honourable scars and worthy battler distinctions, were yesterday, on the Main Street of their home town, while engaged in the patriotic duty of protecting the peace, the victims of murderous assaults by riotous aliens. One of these returned soldiers, who won the Victoria Cross on the battlefields of France, narrowly escaped death as the result of the activities of two of our Austrian residents—no doubt registered alien enemies. There is not a returned soldier in Winnipeg, whatever his views on the strike, who will not thrill with anger at the audacity of these aliens.

Porter's last dispatch in the *Vancouver Sun* appeared on June 12 under the headline "Arrival of Robertson May Mean Action Soon Against Strike Heads."

The arrival of Senator Robertson, minister of labor, tonight is expected to bring up the question of serving warrants on strike leaders for which plans were completed last week. Srgt. Coppins V.C. is recovering in hospital. The soldiers are furious over the fact that he was nearly beaten to death by aliens in the mob. Mounted squadrons are being drilled constantly while nearly three thousand special police with pistols will be on the streets tomorrow. The patience of the citizens is exhausted and the mob in future is to be treated with every force necessary to break resistance.

On June 13, the *Citizen*'s editor hinted at imminent action against the strike leadership in "An Awakening Is Coming."

The leadership of the present so-called general strike in Winnipeg can no longer keep up the pretence that this is strike and not revolution. The strike bulletin

A Few Frank Words Concerning Agitators

Where do all the agitators who are so persistent in telling the honest workman that he is a down-trodden wage slave, come from?

Who made them agitators in the first place and are they competent men to be leaders of the workers?

We have the authority of the Maimi Herald for the statement that Agitator Bray was a butcher in that town and a subtle remark that in the Soviet government he ought to take the portfolio as minister of the evading of debts.

Agitator Armstrong, who is loudly persistent in telling the workers that they are "poor fools" and that they should rise up and take what rightly belongs to them — the industries, never figured in any industrial movement unless it was a movement to tie up industry by calling a strike.

Agitator Blumberg, the man who is keenly interested in turning "wage slaves" into auto-mobile owners and two-hour-a-day-and-half-day-off on Saturday Socialists, is not noted as a worker himself. He is not a wage slave. In fact he never slaves at anything unless it is on a platform with an alien audience where he slaves for an hour in broken English to tell them that they are the salt of the earth and that the earth belongs to them.

Agitator Russell is really secretary and business manager for the Metal Workers but as a fanatical Socialist shouts to high heaven that blood will flow in Winnipeg. It is sure that none of his blood would flow in any case, but his wild words serve to stir up others to fanaticism.

Agitator Johns is of the oily description. He keeps his name as much as possible out of places where it is likely to lead to publicity. Publicity is the last thing on earth he is looking for. He only wants to be left quietly alone to do the real basic work and then disappear before the storm breaks.

Agitator Ivens was a minister, is probably yet a minister of sorts, but finds that certain labor men and women fall for his style of oratory and consequently takes the line of least resistance and stays where he is sure of a few followers. He has an axe of his own to grind and the strikers will find it out. He never was a trades unionist. He never held a union card. He has no real sympathies with labor unions except that he finds them useful to forward his own ideas of running the earth.

It would appear that the principal requisite in an agitator is that he has never done a real day's labor in his life. That he be a crank on some Socialistic scheme to help the useless ones to get ahead of the real workers, and that he have a pet theory to expound, and perhaps put into force.

Passing over the personality of the female agitator Mrs. George Armstrong, who on her own admission spent several years in a lunatic asylum, and who therefore cannot be counted on to be extraordinarily well balanced, we come to Alderman E. Robinson, Alderman John Queen and Alderman A. A. Heaps. Robinson does not say much but when he does say anything it is listened to. His expressions get redder and redder as the days go by and his word has previously had weight. This makes him more dangerous than the real, out and out "red" agitator. Alderman Heaps is the stormy petrel of the Labor Temple and the council chamber. He makes a great noise, is a trades unionist and works on occasion as an upholsterer. The average opinion of him is that he makes a lot of bullets for Queen to fire and that he is a dangerous revolutionist.

Alderman Queen is not a trades unionist. He does not hold a union card. No person in Winnipeg recalls the time when he ever did a day's work. He lives, presumably, on the $1,200 paid him by his own vote as an alderman of Winnipeg. His trade is sowing trouble for some other poor simpletons to reap. His words and actions have brought trades unionism into disrepute and the opinion that some real labor men hold of him is not fit for publication.

Advertisement in the *Winnipeg Citizen*, June 16.

Ben Batsford's cartoon in the *Manitoba Free Press*, June 14.

issued yesterday exulted in the straight defiance of constituted authority…This boasting of defiance…is an open claim that the Soviet of James street controls this city and that the proper civic government has been in effect deposed. No matter what measures may be necessary. They must be taken to prove to the agitators and Bolsheviks at the Labor Temple that they are wrong and this country is to be governed by British law and not by Russian Bolshevik law.

The next day, the *Free Press* ran a cartoon on the editorial page by reporter/illustrator Benjamin Batsford. Although Batsford was not allowed a byline on any of his strike reporting, he did sign the drawing. The cartoon depicted a burning torch symbolizing democracy or British constitutional law and a bearded man labeled "BOLSHEVIM" attempting to blow out the flame. The illustration was captioned, "The Torch that Cannot Be Blown Out."

RED FLAG
OR
UNION JACK?

The active leadership of this strike is Red---its most active followers are undesirable aliens---can you support either element?

Choose---Citizens of Winnipeg and Canada---because today is the
time when you MUST decide.

In the Federal House on June 12th, 1919, F. B. Stacey of West-
minster District, British Columbia, stated:

> "Free Trade is not the vital question in the West. The one
> great thought is whether the Union Jack would float over Cana-
> dian cities or the red flag of revolution."

Mr. Stacey summed up Bolshevism, the I. W. W. and the One Big
Union as being "the same thing over different form."

Some of you have not yet wakened to the fact that this social war
is planned to disrupt Canada---to break down all industry---to
create that Russian chaos called Bolshevism.

You don't believe it? You think it is exaggerated? That it can't
happen in this 20th century! Neither could the great war---
' but it did!

LISTEN:

These few extracts from an article in the Saturday
Evening Post of May 24th tell the story:

> "Why, in the name of Heaven, should we import ideas of liv-
> ing and social and economic conditions from people who are dis
> satisfied and fleeing from the only ones they know about? We
> are curious fools about some things and this idea of importing
> other peoples' troubles and mistakes is one of them. Now a lot of
> wild asses tell us we are bourgeois and proletariat and capitalist
> ridden, and preach the 'revolution'.
> "The socialistic-anarchist-bolshevistic-anti-bourgeois-to-hell-
> in-a-bunch-with-everything programme is having full swing over
> a large part of Europe these days."

Do you like it?

Will you try some of it here?

It hasn't made good anywhere. Therefore, say its prophets and
well-wishers, it must be just the thing for us!

STILL DON'T BELIEVE IT?

> Rev. Ivens said "Winnipeg is now governed by a Soviet—the
> seat of authority has now been transferred from the City Hall to
> the Labor Temple." Do you want Ivens' dream to come true?
> R. B. Russell said, "The blood that is spilled in Canada will
> depend on the working class." He declared that "the only gov-
> ernmental system in which he believed was the Soviet System as
> they had it in Russia." Do you want this to happen?

These two men, especially Russell, are acknowledged leaders of
the Reds here.

Let Us Be Canadians, First!

CITIZENS' COMMITTEE OF ONE THOUSAND.

Citizens advertisement in the
Manitoba Free Press, June 16.

On June 15, the *Chicago Tribune* ran a dispatch from Evans headlined
"Winnipeg Soviet Dying of Venom in Its Own Fangs" in which he
compared the conflict in Winnipeg to class warfare. "Canada's sympathetic
strike has developed into an endurance contest between the 'middle class'
and the extremists, who are seeking 'proletarian dictatorship' and the
overthrow of the present industrial system...It shows what the bourgeois,
the largest class in the community, and the one which the extremists

attack the hardest, can do when it organizes. It's practically a soviet of the middle class."

The following day, Plewman met with strike leader Bob Russell in the Labor Temple. In a story that would appear on June 17 in the *Star*, Plewman described their meeting.

> *He was very busy, but finally agreed to see me at twelve noon which I did, meeting him at the strike committee's headquarters, a room twelve by twenty-five on the ground floor...Even then Russell had not studied the* [Running Trades Mediation Committee] *proposal and he read it over carefully while I waited, and then expressed the opinion that it did not provide for iron masters meeting business agents and not their employes* [sic] *as obtained on the railways. He said that the strike would go on until the men gained all their demands including reinstatement of everybody. He thought the other side was squealing.*

CHAPTER 4
MIDNIGHT ARRESTS

June 17–18

In the early hours of June 17, six strike leaders, including Ivens and Russell, and four foreigners were arrested on charges of seditious conspiracy. They were transported to Stoney Mountain Penitentiary, twenty miles north of Winnipeg. An arrest warrant was also issued for Vancouver labour organizer William Pritchard. At the same time, the James Street Labor Temple, Liberty Hall and Ukrainian Labor Temple were raided by RNWMP and hundreds of special police for evidence of seditious conspiracy. During the early evening, Plewman interviewed James Woodsworth at the Labor Temple. By the end of the day, Woodsworth and Fred Dixon had assumed direction of the *Labor News*. Winnipeg authorities now had at their disposal a force of 245 RNWMP officers, 1,500 special police and more than 2,000 militia.

On June 18, Alfred Andrews announced that the arrested men would be held for deportation proceedings in line with the amended Immigration Act and refused bail. In Ottawa, Tom Moore, president of the Dominion Trades and Labor Congress, condemned the "strong-arm methods for the suppression of legitimate labor demonstrations" and threatened to hold the government strictly accountable "if the proof is not sufficient to show the Winnipeg labor leaders were plotting danger to the state." There was

Arrested strike leaders at the Vaughan Street jail, 1920. *Back row, left to right*: Roger Bray, George Armstrong, Alderman John Queen, R.B. Russell, R.J. Johns and William Pritchard. *Front row, left to right*: William Ivens and Alderman Abraham Heaps. *Courtesy of Archives of Manitoba N12322, Winnipeg Strike 35.*

mixed reaction by newspaper editors to the arrests. Limited streetcar service resumed in Winnipeg.

Under the banner "Winnipeg Strike Leaders Are Arrested" on June 17, the *Star* ran Plewman's account of the "midnight arrests," as well as his interview with James Woodsworth. The paper headlined his main story "Ivens, Russell and Bray Now Held by the Police."

> *A sensation was sprung in Winnipeg at an early hour to-day, when men, who are supposed to be the leaders of the general strike movement, were arrested in the quiet of their homes by hundreds of mounted police and special constables. The arrested men include R.B. Russell, secretary of the Metal Trades Council and an international officer, and credited with being*

one of the dominating factors in the strike; Rev. Wm. Ivens, editor of the Western Labor News, the strike paper, and pastor of the Labor Church that has been holding open air meetings in the parks on Sunday nights; Ald. John Queen, advertising manager of the Western Labor News, and member of the City Council for Ward Five; Ald. A.A. Heaps, upholsterer, also a member of Ward Five; R.E. Bray, one of the leaders of the striking veterans, and George Armstrong, a streetcar motorman who was prominent at the Calgary convention and had spoken much during the strike at meetings in the parks.

Plewman then provided details on the ransacking of the strikers' headquarters.

Simultaneous with the arrests, the Labor Temple, strikers' headquarters, was raided by the Royal Northwest Mounted police, and literature seized. The building was thoroughly searched and doors and rooms that could not be opened were broken down. Books and papers of all sorts were taken and thrown into waiting automobiles. The raid was conducted by Inspector Green, of the city police force, and Inspector Mead, of the Royal Northwest Mounted Police. For the purpose, a cordon of special police constables, numbering several hundred, were placed around the building. I was at the labor temple at six o'clock to-day, and saw the window in the [front] *door broken clean out. I was told that a dozen redcoats, backed by more than five hundred special constables, had surrounded the building and finding the door locked and the strike committee not in session, as it has been sometimes early in the morning, broke into the building and seized all papers they could find.*

Minutes later, Woodsworth arrived at the Labor Temple, and Plewman seized the opportunity for an interview.

As I was standing outside the building, Woodsworth, the former Methodist Minister and later a longshoreman in Vancouver, who is here assisting the strike and doing some special writing for the Labor News, came hurrying up from the Canadian Pacific Hotel, where he is staying. I asked him what he thought of the authorities' action. He replied: "It is a stupid, high-handed move. Already the workers feel that the Government is not truly representative, that it represents only a section and not all the community." "Will the strike collapse now that the leaders are removed?" he was asked.

J.S. Woodsworth, 1904. *Courtesy of Library and Archives Canada C-055449.*

"Not at all," he replied. "The Government can't arrest thirty-five thousand strikers, and if the strike was broken the people would still insist upon handling their affairs and securing the ancient rights of Britons."

Finally, Plewman suggested who was responsible for the arrests.

The Dominion Government is credited with orders to make all arrests. Senator Robertson, Minister of labor was out most of the night and returned to his hotel room about four this morning, when the arrests were nearly completed. Shortly before he was asked if anything was doing and with a broad smile he answered, "Nothing." Premier Norris tried to see Senator Robertson at mid-night, and finding him out, went to bed. The wholesale arrests here followed long conferences between Premier Norris, Mayor Gray, General Ketchen and Lieut-Col. Starnes, head of the Mounted Police, held on Friday night until after midnight, at the Royal Alexandra Hotel and again yesterday morning at the Legislative Buildings. A.J. Andrews, KC, was much in evidence last night.

Editorial reaction to the arrests was mixed. In "Against Strong Arm Measures," published on June 17 but written prior to the arrests, Dafoe had cautioned against premature action by the authorities.

The Free Press has been explicit in declaring its attitude toward every phase of the general strike as it has proceeded. There has been no question as to where it stood at each successive development. In keeping with its record, the Free Press now proposes to say in the clearest terms it can command, that it emphatically dissociates itself from any strong arm policy of breaking the strike. There have been rumors for some days of possible developments along this line and at this moment there are reports of impending operations of this nature. The Free Press declares, that in its judgment, actions of this character would have an effect diametrically opposite to that which its promoters attribute to it. It would complicate an already intricate situation: it would prolong and embitter the strike.

Nevertheless, Dafoe felt that responsibility to end the strike still rested with "Red leaders."

The strike situation, as the Free Press has set forth repeatedly, is that the labor bodies of Winnipeg have been misled by Red leaders, who have usurped power, into an impossible and disastrous position…The roots of this strike folly had gone so deep that it required time to reach them. The process has been tedious and trying, but it has been effective, and it requires only persistence for a comparatively short additional period of time to bring about the collapse of the general strike under conditions which will guarantee industrial peace in Winnipeg for a long time to come.

The next day, Dafoe reacted to the authorities' intervention in "The Arrests." After describing the jailed men as "leaders of a senseless, criminal strike which was nearing collapse," he cautioned that the arrests "may do the extremists an actual service" and "enable them to pose as martyrs in the cause of the workingman." Nevertheless, he supported the authorities' actions. "The Dominion Government…possibly has information not available to the public which compelled the action it has taken. It may be justified by the results obtained. The Government has taken its course; it must see it through."

The *Tribune*'s Moncrieff responded with "The Arrests—A Fair Trial Awaited."

The most radical step taken by the Dominion authorities since the outbreak of the strike was the arrest, at an early hour this morning, of a number of men whose names, have been prominently identified with the leadership of the strike…Whether the action leading to the arrest has been wise or unwise will depend wholly on the evidence…An immediate trial of the men under arrest must take place. The establishment of their guilt, or otherwise, will depend upon sworn testimony and such documentary evidence as the authorities have in their possession.

The next day, Moncrieff added the carefully worded "Most Serious Charges."

The assumption must be that the Dominion Government has ample and specific evidence that the men under arrest have violated the laws of Canada…When the highest authority in the Dominion places its hands on any man or men residing in Canada, citizens, including newspaper editors, who are not in the immediate confidence of the authorities and having no definite knowledge of the evidence leading to the arrest, can only withhold comment pending knowledge which will enable men making comment to exercise their own judgment in the premises. Whether the action leading to the arrests has been wise or unwise, will depend wholly on the evidence.

The Tribune appeals for calmness on the part of all good citizens. An immediate fair trial must take place.

In contrast, on June 17, in the front-page commentary "Now for the Hand of Steel," Magee completely supported the arrests.

At last we have start of action. At last we have officialdom aroused to a sense of duty. At last we have the first move of those in authority to pick up the challenge cast down by treason and to exert the pressure of the strong arm of the law…Let any man and every man who is fool enough to get in the way and to attempt to deprive the people of their rights be subjected to the consequences of his folly. Let him either be removed without loss and fuss and theatrical nonsense to a place of detention and punishment, or let him be crushed in the streets as an example of warning to others, who may be tempted to follow his example…Let there be no faltering now. Let there be no half measure now.

On the same day, under the banner headline "KEEP COOL—DO NOTHING WE'VE GOT THEM BEAT NOW," the *Labor News'* new co-editor Fred Dixon[19] reacted to the authorities' actions with "Who Is Responsible for the Outrage?" He began with details of Ivens's arrest.

A young Canadian wife and mother (Mrs. Ivens), sobbed out her story. Nervously unstrung, almost hysterical, she closed her eyes to try to shut out the vision of a band of men who had broken into her room and carried off her husband without even permitting to learn of the crime with which he was charged. She feared they would beat him up or do away with him. Yes, some of them were in uniform, but no real officers of the law would act as those men acted…Little children still in their night clothes, looked on half in fear, half in wonder. Little had she thought that her husband—a Christian minister—would be treated as the most dangerous of criminals. Is this Canada? Is this British law?

Then he described the results of the raid on the strikers' headquarters.

In the early morning hours, the Labor Temple presented a sorry spectacle. Glass windows of the doors had been broken—supposedly by duly constituted officers of the law. A cigar stand…had been looted and boxes and cigars which had escaped the raiders were strewn about the table and floor…Various offices were wrecked. Apparently an axe or crow bar had

Western Labor News
SPECIAL STRIKE EDITION No. 27 EXTRA

Published by the Strike Committee, Labor Temple.	Price 5 cents.	Winnipeg, Man., Tuesday, June 17th, 1919.

KEEP COOL–DO NOTHING
WE'VE GOT THEM BEAT NOW

Western Labor News, June 17.

> been used to break open the doors, to smash drawers and desks and generally execute as much damage as possible. Papers, correspondence, file records and supplies were strewn about the floor...

Finally, Dixon asked who was responsible.

> Who does know, is the question that the citizen worker is asking. Who is responsible for the outrage? Was the setting and acting under the authority of the Dominion Government? Where did Provincial and city authorities come in?...The papers seem to know. We are as yet simply finding out. All we can say as yet is: Missing—R.E. Bray, R.B. Russell, Rev. Wm. Ivens, Ald. John Queen. Ald. A.A. Heaps, Geo. Armstrong.

The next day, Dixon's co-editor, Woodsworth, criticised the Citizens in "Fools and Knaves."

> "Whom the Gods would destroy they first make mad." When the knaves on the Committee of 1000 started the villainous campaign which has resulted in the arrest of six of the most devoted men who ever served the cause of labor, they fondly and falsely imagined that by securing the arrest of these men they could break the strike...All the miserable tactics of the 1000 have failed of their main purpose. They have failed to break the strike. They have failed to prevent the strike from spreading...They will be taught that 35,000 brains and hearts are united and these brains and hearts will in the long run rise victorious through all the nefarious machinations of the 1000, secure the objects for which this strike is being waged and vindicate the men who were arrested on Tuesday morning.

Also on June 18, Plewman wrote a follow-up dispatch headlined "Arrest of Leaders May Consolidate Strikers." The story featured a picture of Arthur Meighen with the caption, "Hon. Arthur Meighen who is credited with originating and carrying out Winnipeg coup by which ten strike leaders were arrested. Provincial and municipal authorities and even other Dominion authorities claim to have been ignorant of the plan. Mr. Meighen is regarded as a great technical lawyer, and has also been acquiring a reputation as a man of 'blood and iron' in the Cabinet." According to Plewman, the arrests had not discouraged the strikers. "Nearly every strike and labor leader to whom I have spoken…seemed to believe that the arrests had consolidated the strikers and made them feel more deeply that constituted authority represented financial interests and not the common people. They all intimated that the strike would go on with greater determination than ever."

CHAPTER 5
THERE WILL BE BLOOD

JUNE 19-21

On June 19, Ivens was removed by the Methodist Conference of Manitoba from its roll of ordained ministers. According to a report in the *Montreal Herald*, nineteen streetcars were back in operation in Winnipeg. On June 19 and 20, Robertson met with Strike Committee moderates, including James Winning, to end the strike. The next day, the final issue of the *Citizen* was published. At an evening meeting in Market Square, pro-strike veterans decided to have a "silent parade" the next day starting in front of City Hall at 2:30 p.m. and marching to the Royal Alexandra Hotel to confront Gideon Robertson. General Ketchen informed his superiors in Ottawa that he was prepared to deal with any situation arising from the planned demonstration. At 6:40 p.m., William Pritchard was arrested on a westbound CPR train in Calgary by RNWMP.

During the morning of June 21, six arrested strike leaders, including Ivens and Russell, were released on bail from Stoney Mountain. As a condition of their release, the men pledged to no longer take a role in the strike, including public speaking or newspaper interviews. In advance of the "silent parade," Mayor Gary issued his third proclamation against public gatherings, including a warning to women.

The proclamation issued by me some days ago must be strictly adhered to. It has been brought to my attention that a parade of men, women and children is proposed for today. I hereby reiterate my former proclamation that there shall be no parades until the end of the strike. Any women taking part in a parade do so at their own risk.

Less than thirty minutes before the planned silent parade, Plewman interviewed Robertson in the Royal Alexandra Hotel. Beginning at 2:30 p.m., several thousand pro-labour veterans, strikers, strike sympathizers and onlookers were confronted near City Hall by 50 RNWMP, 1,200 special police and 2,000 militia.[20] For the best view and for personal safety, photographers and most reporters stationed themselves on rooftops. However, Canadian Press Winnipeg bureau manager J.F.B. Livesay remained at street level. Violence ensued after Mayor Gray read the Riot Act. In the confrontation, one man was killed, more than thirty were injured and dozens were arrested. In "Hell's Alley," a lane between Market and James Avenue, twenty-seven others were injured. The riot was subsequently labeled "Bloody Saturday" by Fred Dixon in the *Labor News*.

The last issue of the *Citizen* was published on June 20. To reemphasize the revolutionary nature of the strike, the editor wrote "Let Us Settle It Now."

When this revolution was attempted, when union labor was induced to throw its weight against civilization and civil rights, the declaration of the Soviet was "this is a fight to the finish." The citizens accepted the challenge…There must be no weakening now…The people who ruthlessly tried to cast this city back into conditions of the middle ages must be made to pay the price…They have been told that those who persisted in striking on the alleged "sympathetic plea" would not be re-engaged except where found convenient.

There was also advice for employers. "Employers will not now break faith with men and women who came to the rescue of the public services in the hour of need. They will re-employ strikers where convenient, but not otherwise…Such a concession would only invite the renewal of similar tactics at another time in the not distant future when the Bolshevists again consider the time ripe to strike."

On the same day, the *Chicago Tribune* ran Evans's final dispatch from Winnipeg.

> *The further one looks into Canada's sympathetic strike the more conceived it becomes that: The great bull of labor is sound as a bell and is not behind the program of the radical leaders. A comparatively few revolutionaries who came into power through alien support while the fighting men were in France, are running the show. The one big union idea, which proposes to tell the bell for trades unionism to overthrow the present industrial system and establish the soviet form of communism and class control, is the real issue.*

During the evening of June 20, Plewman attended the meeting of several thousand pro-strike veterans in Market Square. The next day, the *Star* ran his account of the event under the headline "Veterans in 'Peg Are Threatening to Force Issue."

> *"If the Government won't settle the strike, returned soldiers will," shouted Comrade Parnell, successor to R.E. Bray, arrested leader of the striking veterans, to a meeting called under their auspices in the Market Square last night. A crowd of twelve thousand, one-fifth of whom were veterans, enthusiastically cheered the announcement. "Our veterans' committee worked all afternoon trying to help a settlement," declared Parnell. "We've worked for weeks and the Government has done nothing. We won't stand for inaction any longer. Saturday afternoon at 2:30 we will hold a monster silent indignation parade, which is the most effective of weapons." The significance of this declaration is that street parades are under the ban and the civil authorities, backed by the Provincial and Federal authorities have absolutely committed themselves to the breaking up of any such demonstrations. Veterans preceding Parnell stated that the time had come for "mass action" with brains and brawn, which they had found so effective in Flanders. "I don't mean rough stuff," he added quickly. "If there are any barriers keep calm and remain silent. This is not the time for rough stuff."*

After reporting that Parnell "roughly denounced the Minister of Labor, who[m] he argued was committed to a policy of starving the workers until the strike had been beaten," Plewman noted, "Winnipeg is full of rumors that the striking veterans are going to forcibly stop the [street] cars and seize various public places, but the labor leaders say they are doing their best to restrain the returned men."

Plewman ended the dispatch with a summary of strike developments.

Market Square, circa 1919. *Courtesy of Gary Becker Collection, Heritage Winnipeg.*

"Evidence that material progress towards a settlement was made on Thursday is not forthcoming. The returned men are very insistent that the railway mail clerks, postal employes [*sic*] and dismissed policemen shall be reinstated. A Living wage is not at issue. The back of the collective bargaining issue appears broken, and reinstatement appears to be the big question."

Finally, in an editorial published before the afternoon riot of June 21, Magee criticized the government's decision to release six arrested strike leaders from Stony Mountain Prison.

> *The Federal Government's badge is blue. The badge of the Bolshevists is red. The Government is supposed to be a true blue Government. Those revolutionaries who were arrested and sent to Stony Mountain the other morning boast of being "Reds." Sandpaper both of these worthy bodies, and their true color is revealed—a brilliant yellow! After making a theatrical display—which is only revealed as theatrical because of the farcical aftermath—after arresting the ringleaders in the attempted rebellion and spiriting them away to the penitentiary, the Government has entered into negotiations with the very men that it accused of some of the most serious crimes of which anyone could be guilty…This is such a pitiable farce, such a miserable fiasco, that one is in doubt whether to curse or to laugh at it…The citizens of Winnipeg have not failed, and they will not fail. The Federal Government has failed abjectly—and failed because of no*

lack of understanding of the trickery of political expediency.

THE RIOT OF JUNE 21

As planned, during the early afternoon of June 21, hundreds of returned soldiers began congregating along Main Street and William Avenue. Combined with strikers, their supporters and bystanders, the crowd in the vicinity of City Hall and Market Square numbered several thousand. Meanwhile, Robertson was still chairing a meeting that had begun in the Royal Alexandra Hotel at 10:00 a.m. The purpose of the conference—involving Robertson, Andrews, Mayor Gray, RNWMP commissioner Perry and a committee of three pro-strike veterans, plus a member of the Strike Committee—was to find a way to prevent the parade.

When it became apparent that the march would not be cancelled, Gray left the meeting to assess developments near City Hall. Shortly after 2:00 p.m., Robertson and the veterans emerged into the hotel's lobby, where Plewman was waiting to learn their next moves. In "Over Eighty Arrests Follow Riots in 'Peg," he described what transpired next.

> *As the committee left the hotel, they told me their plans were not defined and five of them stood hesitatingly in discussion in the middle of the road while two others were taken in Andrew's automobile to see whether an arrangement could be made for the veterans to hold meetings in the Industrial Bureau. A few minutes after the veterans left, Senator Robertson told me that his offer to speak to the veterans in Victoria Park had been rejected because he was not able to announce a strike settlement. The veterans deny this, but admit that they called upon Mayor Gray to resign.*

Twenty-five minutes after Plewman's interview with Robertson, violence erupted in front of City Hall. Canadian Press Winnipeg bureau manager Fred Livesay was eyewitness to events and subsequently provided newspapers across the country with an exclusive story. His dispatch was wired to the west coast in time for the *Vancouver Daily Province* to run the story the same day; eastern papers had to wait until Monday, June 23.[21] The *Province* ran Livesay's entire scoop on the front page.

Riot Act Is Read in Winnipeg; Police Charge; One Killed
Firearms Reported to Have Been Used by R.N.W.M.P. and Special Constables in Conflict with Mob

A crowd gathering at Main Street and William Avenue at about 1:45 p.m., June 21. *Courtesy of Archives of Manitoba N2771, Foote 1705.*

Inspector Proby's mounted force on Portage Avenue approaching Main Street at about 2:30 p.m., June 21. *Courtesy of Archives of Manitoba N2756, Foote 1690.*

Paraded Despite Mayor's Warning
Crowd Wrecks Street Car in Front of the City Hall—Missiles Are
Thrown by Strikers

(By Canadian Press)

Winnipeg, June 21—Mayor Gray has read the Riot Act.[22]
   Northwest Mounted Police and special police charged on the street three times. Missiles were thrown by strikers.
   A street car was wrecked by the mob, who is attempting to overturn it in front of the City Hall.
   It has been unofficially reported that one person has been killed and three injured in the rioting.
   The casualties occurred when the police fired into the crowd. Street car wrecked by mob and is now burning.

Winnipeg, June 21—Winnipeg went under martial law at 3 o'clock this afternoon when the Riot Act was read. But not before one man had been killed and two others wounded by revolver shots in their defense by mounted

Mounties moving north on Main Street shortly after 2:30 p.m., June 21. *Courtesy of Archives of Manitoba N2760, Foote 1694.*

Mounties charging north on Main Street, June 21. *Courtesy of Archives of Manitoba N2757, Foote 1691.*

police. Mike Sokolwoki [sic], 552 Henry Street, registered alien, was shot right through the heart as, it is claimed, he was crossing from one side of William Avenue to the other at the time the Royal North-West Mounted Police made their charge.[23]

At the same time Robert C. Johnstone, 548 Ross Avenue, returned soldier, who had served three and a half years with the 5th Canadian Infantry Battalion, was shot through the left thigh, the bullet entering the right knee. The other man injured was Jack Barrett, a young fellow, who was looking on and claims he had no other interest than that of a spectator. He was shot through the right thigh. Both men will recover.

20,000 IN CROWD

The tragic events of the afternoon covered not more than half an hour. At 2:30 p.m. perhaps 20,000 persons were massed on Main street with their focus at City Hall. For the most part they appeared to be strikers, with among them several thousand returned soldiers, and they were congregated to witness or take part in the "massed silent parade," which it was announced last night in the meeting at the Market Square of returned soldiers would be put on by returned soldiers alone this afternoon as a last final effort to break down the barriers the men claimed to have been erected against the propaganda of the general strike in Winnipeg.

On the whole this great mass was orderly. It contained many women, evidently of the strikers' families, but no children. Shortly before 2:30 a small riot developed on Market street just east of City Hall park around a man who was drunk. Leaders of the crowd asked the men involved to be quiet as they would spoil by their rowdyism the whole effect of the silent demonstration.

STREET CAR INCIDENT

At 2:35 o'clock a street car passing on Main street only made its way through the crowds amidst continual booing and with great difficulty, the trolley several times being pulled off the line. Evidently regarding the whole thing as a circus a great stream of citizens in their automobiles passed at this critical moment up and down Main street, by no means adding to the good feeling of what was fast developing into an angry mob.

A crowd trying to tip streetcar #596 in front of City Hall, June 21. *Courtesy of Archives of Manitoba N2762, Foote 1696.*

Mounties turn onto William Avenue before their final charge, June 21. *Courtesy of William Wilson.*

Smoldering streetcar #596 in front of City Hall, June 21. *Courtesy of Archives of Manitoba N2763, Foote 1696.*

"FALL IN" ORDER

Sharp at 2:30 the word passed along and the crowd gathered in the wide thoroughfare of Main street on each side of the car tracks, "fall in."

At that very moment Portage Avenue car No. 596 appeared from the north, about half full of passengers, mostly women and children. As it reached Market Street it was greeted by a rolling roar of booing, its trolley was pulled off the line and some stones were thrown. Women and children got out of the car and dispersed among the crowd, so far as known, unhurt. The conductor and motorman remained by their car, the trolley cord having been cut, it remaining a fixture at what immediately was to become a scene of battle.

Almost simultaneously with this stunt the cry went out from the crowd: "Here comes the bloody soldiers," and around the corner of Main street from the south, opposite the Union Bank, swept a single line of red-coated Royal North West Mounted Police. They covered the wide street from gutter to gutter, passing around the street car.

RETURNED R.N.W.M.P.

Immediately an angry cry was heard from the mob and an occasional missile was thrown at the passing soldiers. A hundred yards behind this first rank came a second rank of khaki-clad horsemen, said by the crowd to be members of the Strathcona Horse and the Fort Garry Horse., but afterwards stated by Mayor Gray to be R.N.W.M.P men returned from the front to whom had not been issued the well-known scarlet tunic.

The mob surged in on the flanks of the horsemen and a free throwing of bricks, bottles and any other available missiles began, many of the horsemen being struck. They rode on however, north several blocks and then after a short interval returned with drawn truncheons and, driving up into two columns of four on each side of the street, sought to drive the mob back onto the sidewalks.

THE PROCLAMATION

Following is the proclamation issued this morning by Mayor Gray warning citizens against taking part in this afternoon's parade, which was decided on at a meeting in Market Square yesterday.

"The proclamation issued by me some days ago must be strictly adhered to. It has been brought to my attention that a parade of men, women and children is proposed for today. I hereby reiterate my former proclamation that there shall be no parades until the end of the strike. Any women taking part in a parade do so at their own risk."

Between four and five thousand took part in the meeting in the Market Square, all the speakers being veterans. It was an orderly gathering except for the booing at every reference to the special policemen.

Call was made at the meeting for the disbandment of the Winnipeg

Special police cordon across Main Street near Market Avenue at about 3:45 p.m., June 21. *Courtesy of Archives of Manitoba N2768, Foote 1702.*

General Ketchen's militia with mounted machine guns on Main Street, June 21. *Courtesy of Archives of Manitoba N2770, Foote 1704.*

Militia and mounties holding Main Street, June 21. *Courtesy of Archives of Manitoba N2764, Foote 1698.*

Citizens' Committee and this was accompanied by a demand that the convention hall in the Board of Trade Building be thrown open to meetings of the returned men.

In his autobiography, Livesay detailed how he obtained his scoop.[24]

When the shooting started there was a double movement; as if reaped by a scythe, the old soldiers lay down, while the rest, men, women and children, streamed like quicksilver into the neighbouring courts and alleys. One of these, an [sic] Ukrainian friend, shouted out to me as he ran by: "Get out of here, Mr. Livesay, they're shooting with real bullets!" Like plumes and whorls of wind-driven clouds disappearing in mountain clefts…two concentric movements; in a moment the square was clear. Even the troops had passed on, and I stood alone, lord of all I surveyed; a dead man lay before me…Before help came, and my man was carried into an undertaker's parlour, I reached into his pocket for his alien registration card and slipped it into my own wallet. Now indeed I had a scoop and it looked time to get going. All street-car traffic had been suspended, and I ran a mile or more to the office. There, in the next hour, I dictated to Harold Raine the story, and he hammered it out, handing it sheet by sheet to the Morse operator, whence it was laid down in St. Paul and thence fanned out over the continent. Local papers, well behind us with the story, for their reporters had watched the melee from high buildings fronting on Main Street, were skeptical about the names of my dead, and did not use the item in that extra nor until I had leisurely explained. I regretted having to turn over the identification card to the police.

Livesay then described how he returned to the scene of the riot and fooled Garnet Porter.

It was time to get back to the fray, but what a difference! All Main Street was corded off, lined with troops, and with fussy officers barring the way. "Let that man through!" said my old friend, Colonel G.C. Porter. "He's a newspaperman, Canadian Press…Fred," he went on as I passed the cordon, "this is a great story and I'm just going to file my stuff." He was a free-lance stringing for a number of Canadian and American papers. "What have you got?" "What have I got?" I replied, carelessly. "I'm beginning to look around now." On Monday [June 23] *we met in Mariaggi's bar. "Fred," he said, "you certainly scooped me that time! They turned back on me thousands and thousands of words, saying the CP story stood up all day. Good for you!"…So we had another* [drink].

CHAPTER 6
LET US REASON TOGETHER

JUNE 22–28

On June 23, Mayor Gray issued a final proclamation clearly directed at pro-labour veterans, strikers and foreigners.

PROCLAMATION

The Riot Act has been read and remains in full force and effect in Winnipeg.

Riotous assembly of crowds, riotous attack on persons or property, riotous damaging of property are indictable offences and all persons guilty of same are liable to imprisonment.

Assembly in crowds, congregating and standing in the streets is dangerous, and you do so at your own risk.

The riots of Saturday were a direct challenge to constituted authority, and were promptly and vigorously suppressed and my Proclamation strictly enforced.

Citizens—All lawlessness and intimidation must cease

Those of you who wish to return to work can do so without fear of molestation, and if you are in the slightest way interfered with or intimidated, notify at once the Mayor or Chief of Police and the offenders will be traced down by the Royal North-West Mounted Police and City Police, if it takes years to do so.

Any foreigners who make any threats of any kind or in any way intimidate or worry would be workers in the slightest degree can expect immediate deportation to Russia or wherever they came from. We intend to purge this city of any lawless element and prosecute to the full rigor of the law. On the other hand, all law abiding citizens can feel free to go about their business in the full realization that British law will protect them to the limit. No further open air meetings, either in parks, streets or public places will be permitted until further notice.

God Save the King

As well, on June 23, Andrews obtained arrest warrants for James Woodsworth and Fred Dixon on charges of seditious libel related to their writings in the *Western Labor News*. Andrews also banned further printing of the strikers' paper. Woodsworth was arrested and brought to the Rupert Street jail. However, Dixon avoided arrest and went into hiding.

On June 24, Dixon published the *Western Star* in place of the *Labor News*. A special Riot Court released forty-four citizens arrested for "riotous assembly" during Bloody Saturday. Each individual was released on bail set at $1,000. Gideon Robertson left Winnipeg for Ottawa. The next day, Dixon, still in hiding, replaced the *Western Star* with the *Enlightener*, and the WTLC notified workers that the strike would officially end on June 26 at 11:00 a.m. On June 26, Dixon published the last issue of the *Enlightener*. After forty-two days, the strike officially ended at 11:00 a.m. On the same day, Ivens resumed publication of the *Labor News*, and soon after, Dixon voluntarily surrendered to authorities.

On 23 June, the first publication day after the riot, Dafoe used "The Riots" to place responsibility for the violence on the Strike Committee.

The tragic street happenings of Saturday afternoon were the direct, inevitable outcome of the spirit of contempt for the regular constituted authorities which has been preached and practised for the past five weeks

Western Labor News

SPECIAL STRIKE EDITION No. 32

| Published by the Strike Committee, Labor Temple. | Price 5 cents. | Winnipeg, Man., Monday, June 23rd, 1919. |

STRIKE UNBROKEN

KAISERISM WILL NOT WORK

BLOODY SATURDAY

R.N.W.M.P. MAKE GORY DEBUT—PEACEFUL CITIZENS SHOT WITHOUT WARNING—CITY UNDER MILITARY CONTROL—RETURNED MEN INCENSED—STRIKERS MORE DETERMINED.

One is dead and a number injured, probably thirty or more, as result of the forcible prevention of the "silent parade" which had been planned by returned men to start at 2.30 o'clock last Saturday afternoon. Apparently the bloody business was carefully planned, for Mayor Gray issued a proclamation in the morning stating that "Any women taking part in a parade do so at their own risk." Nevertheless a vast crowd of men, women and children assembled to witness the "silent parade."

The soldiers' committee, which had been interviewing Senator Robertson, had not returned to their comrades when the latter commenced to line up on Main St., near the city hall.

No attempt was made to use the special city police to prevent the parade. On a previous occasion a dozen of the old regular city police had persuaded the returned men to abandon a parade which had commenced to move.

On Saturday, about 2.30 p.m., just the time when the parade was scheduled to start, some 50 mounted men swinging baseball bats rode down Main St. Half were red-coated R.N.W.M.P., the others wore khaki. They quickened pace as they passed the Union Bank. The crowd opened, let them through and closed in behind them. They turned and charged through the crowd again, greeted by hisses, boos, and some stones. There were two riderless horses with the squad when it emerged and galloped up Main St. The men in khaki disappeared at this juncture, but the red-coats reined their horses and reformed opposite the old post office.

the human rights they have fought to defend, and they are especially incensed by the murderous assault of the mounties upon an unarmed crowd. One man, recently returned, said: "They treated us worse than we ever treated Fritzy."

The returned men assumed full responsibility for the "silent parade" proposition, making a special request that the strikers should not join them. "This is our affair," they declared. Had they intended violence they would hardly have invited their wives to join in the parade.

"COLLECTIVE BARGAINING NOT CONCEDED"

Re statement in Western Labor News, Friday, June 21st, 1919, an article, entitled "Strike Still On," the statement is made that the "Principles of collective bargaining is conceded. Definitions are being worked out." The General Strike Committee desire to correct the erroneous ideas which may be conveyed by above statement. A paper was received from Senator Robertson proporting to be what the Metal Masters understood by Collective Bargaining. It was felt by the General Strike Committee that the Metal Trades Employees, those directly effected by this paper, should get in touch with the Iron Masters in order to get their interpretation. They proceeded to interview Senator Robertson, when it was discovered that Senator Robertson's interpretation was directly opposite to the Metal Trades Employees' ideas on this question. Further, he informed them that he had no power to gain them an interview with the Iron Masters, and up to this date we have received no direct communication from the three Iron Masters involved. The Committee considers that it is not merely a matter of definition, and that the principle of collective bargaining has not been conceded.

(Signed) THE STRIKE COMMITTEE.

Kaiserism in Canada

What shall the sacrifice profit Canada if she who has helped to destroy Kaiserism in Germany shall allow Kaiserism to be established at home? Whoever ordered the shooting last Saturday is a Kaiser of the deepest dye.

The responsibility must be placed and the criminal brought before the bar of justice.

There may be those who think that the blood of innocent men upon our streets is preferable to a "silent parade." There may be those who think their dignity must be upheld at any cost. But we fail to see the slightest justification for the murderous assault which was committed. Whoever ordered it acted in the spirit of Kaiser Wilhelm when he said: "Recruits! Before the altar and the servant of God you have given me the oath of allegiance. You are too young to know the full meaning of what you have said, but your first care must be to obey implicitly all orders and directions. You have sworn fidility to me, you are the children of my guard, you are my soldiers, you have surrendered yourselves to me, body and soul. Only one enemy can exist for you—my enemy. With the present Socialist machinations, it may happen that I shall order you to shoot your own relations, your brothers, or even your parents—which God forbid—and then you are bound in duty implicitly to obey my orders."

The events of last week show to what lengths the opponents of labor will go in their efforts to fasten despotism on this city and this country. The midnight arrest of men whose only crime seems to be that of lese majeste against the profiteers, and the shooting of innocent and defenceless citizens mark the depths of desperation to which the Kaiser-like crowd at the Industrial Bureau are prepared to go in order to turn their defeat into a temporary victory.

But they must not be allowed even temporary satisfaction. Organized labor must continue the magnificent fight of the last five weeks until its just and moderate demands are granted. It were better that the whole 35,000 strikers languished in jail;

Western Labor News, June 23.

in this city. The responsibility for the affray belongs to the people who will complain most about it—to those who have been by both open and secret methods, challenging the authority of the Governments...The Strike Committee may disclaim, with all sincerity, the demonstrations of disobedience to city authorities which precipitated Saturday's riot; but this only shows...that by their precept and example, they have unloosed forces which they cannot control.

Meanwhile, Woodsworth and Dixon collaborated on a *Labor News* edition topped with "Strike Unbroken" and "Kaiserism Will Not Work." Dixon authored "Bloody Saturday."

One is dead and a number injured, probably thirty or more, as a result of the forcible prevention of the "silent parade" which had been planned by the returned men to start at 2:30 o'clock last Saturday afternoon. Apparently the bloody business was carefully planned, for Mayor Gray issued a proclamation in the morning stating that "Any women taking part in a parade do so at their own risk." Nevertheless a vast crowd of men, women, and children assembled to witness the "silent parade." The soldiers' committee, which had been interviewing Senator Robertson, had not returned to their comrades when the latter commenced to line up on Main Street, near the city hall. No attempt was made to use the special police to prevent the parade. On a previous occasion a dozen of the old regular city police had persuaded the returned men to abandon a parade which had commenced to move.

Next he described the actions of the RNWMP.

On Saturday about 2:30 p.m. just the time when the parade was scheduled to start, some 50 mounted men swinging baseball bats rode down Main Street. Half were red coated R.N.W.M.P., the others wore khaki. They quickened their pace as they passed the Union Bank. The crowd opened, let them through and closed in behind them. They turned and charged through the crowd again, greeted by hisses, boos, and some stones. There were two riderless horses with the squad when it emerged and galloped up Main Street. The men in khaki disappeared at this juncture, but the red-coats reined their horses and reformed opposite the old post office. Then, with revolvers drawn, they galloped down Main St., and charged right into the crowd on William Ave., firing as they charged. One man, standing on the sidewalk, thought the mounties were firing blank cartridges until a spectator standing beside him dropped with a bullet through his breast. Another standing nearby was shot through the head. We have no exact information about the total number of casualties, but there were not less than thirty. The crowd dispersed as quickly as possible when the shooting began. When the mounties rode back to the corner of Portage and Main after the fray, at least two of them were twirling their reeking tubes high in the air in orthodox Deadwood Dick style. Some individuals apparently opposed to the strike, applauded the man-killers as they rode by. Lines of special police, swinging their big clubs, were then thrown across Main Street and the intersecting thoroughfares. Dismounted red-coats lined up across Portage and Main declaring the city under military control. Khaki-clad men with rifles were stationed on the street corners.

Lastly, he indicated the reaction of returned men.

> *There were no open air meetings on Saturday night, but the central strike committee met as usual and resolved to "carry on" with redoubled vigor. If the city remains under military control, meetings will likely be held outside the city limits. Indignation at the action of the authorities was forcibly expressed by returned men. They feel that the prevention of the parade was an infringement of the human rights they have fought to defend, and they are especially incensed by the murderous assault of the mounties upon an unarmed crowd. One man, recently returned, said: "They treated us worse than we ever treated Fritz." The returned men assumed full responsibility for the "silent parade" proposition, making a special request that the strikers should not join them. "This is our affair," they declared. Had they intended violence they would hardly have invited their wives to join in the parade.*

Woodsworth used "Kaiserism in Canada" to criticize those who suppressed the parade.

> *What shall the sacrifice profit Canada if she who has helped to destroy Kaiserism in Germany should allow Kaiserism to be established at home! Whoever ordered the shooting last Saturday is a Kaiser of the deepest dye. The responsibility must be placed and the criminal brought before the bar of justice. There may be those who think that the blood of innocent men upon our streets is preferable to a "silent parade." There may be those who think their dignity must be upheld at any cost. But we fail to see the slightest justification for the murderous assault which was committed. Whoever ordered it acted in the spirit of Kaiser Wilhem.*

Then he encouraged labour to continue the strike.

> *The events of last week show to what lengths the opponents of labor will go in their efforts to fasten despotism on this city and this country. The midnight arrest of men whose only crime seems to be that of lese majeste against the profiteers, and the shooting of innocent and defenceless citizens mark the depths of desperation to which the Kaiser-like crowd at the Industrial Bureau are prepared to go in order to turn their defeat into victory. But they must not be allowed even temporary satisfaction. Organized labor must continue the magnificent fight of the last five weeks until its just and moderate demands are granted. It were better than the whole 35,000 strikers*

languished in jail; better even, that we all rested beside the men who were slain on Saturday, then that the forces of Kaiserism shall prevail. There have always been those who have imagined that "a whiff of grape shot" would stop the cry of the people for justice. There are those in Winnipeg who think the shooting on Saturday taught labor a lesson. The parade was attempted and the blood of innocent men spilled "without permission of the strike committee." Labor already knew that two dozen men on horseback shooting to kill could disperse a crowd of several thousand unarmed men and women.

Finally, Woodsworth censured the Citizens. "The committee of one thousand has, however, many lessons to learn—among other things the members of that committee must be taught that ideas are more powerful then bullets. The blood of the martyrs is the seed of the church. We shall 'carry on' in spite of hell, till victory is won."

By the end of the day, Woodsworth had been arrested on charges of seditious libel and placed in a cell at the Rupert Street police station. Meanwhile, warned by Strike Committee members at the Labor Temple that there was a warrant for his arrest, Dixon had gone into hiding.

Also on June 23, the *Star* ran a dispatch by Plewman headlined "Three Classes with One Big Union Plan." In this report, Plewman described the three types of OBU supporters.

Some high officials here believe there is evidence to support the theory that a wide-spread movement is afoot to overthrow our democratic institutions and substitute for them a Soviet form of government. They allege that the means to that end is to be the One Big Union…Supporters of the One Big Union do not at all feel themselves committed to the same program. They seem to be made up of three classes. 1. Those who would use the One Big Union to secure a larger share of profits of industry and by solidifying the vote of the workers obtain a larger influence in democratic Parliaments…2. Those who use the One Big Union to secure control of Parliamentary bodies and by a combination of strike and political action socialize all productive industry…3. Those who would organize along I.W.W. lines and hasten Soviet rule by resort to violence.

He also commented on the authorities' allegation of evidence of a plot to overthrow the government.

The authorities here believe they have evidence which shows that a genuine revolutionary move is under way to seize control of the country's affairs. They are also convinced that the movement is assisted or even directed from Germany and that money is being forwarded to Canada through German-American banks….Needless to say if evidence of this sort can be brought out Canada is in for a genuine sensation.

Magee wrote several editorials after the June 21 riot. On June 24, in "Stepped Upon," he praised the suppression of the *Labor News* by Andrews and, in "Punish the Guilty Ones," observed that "the men who allowed hordes of aliens to join them in that attempted parade were inviting bloodshed when they did so." The next day, he wrote "The End of the Revolution." "Let us remember the attempt to starve babies, to cause invalids to die, to prevent our homes being kept sanitary, to cause our streets to remain polluted with filth to the jeopardy of our lives; let us remember the thousands of cases of intimidation that have been endured, the thousand-and-one unclassifiable annoyances that we have suffered."

On June 24, Dafoe contributed "Settling the Strike."

The strike was settled yesterday to a very considerable extent by the return of many hundreds of workmen to their occupations. Having reached the very sound conclusion that the strike committee cannot settle the strike they attended to the business themselves…An equally large number of workmen will, in all probability, do their strike-settling today; and in turn their example will be followed by others who from day to day until the only people left on strike will be the strike committee. No doubt months hence, after everybody else has put the strike aside as a disagreeable memory, the strike committee will still be issuing the daily defiance of all and sundry and its daily prediction of an early and sweeping victory.

On the same day, Moncrieff penned "End of the Strike."

The Sympathetic strike is practically at an end. It was inevitable that the strike should soon terminate. Arrayed against it was a great body of well organized Union Labor…Stronger still…was the stand of that most influential and potential of all bodies, the General Public. The moment an attack was made on the public utilities of the city and province and even on the postal service of the nation, the General Public's mind was made up…Under ordinary conditions the Sympathetic Strike would have been a grave mistake. With the hand of Sovietism behind it, it was a very serious blunder and worse, an attack, indeed upon the very institutions of the nation.

In hiding, Dixon published the *Western Star.*[25] The June 24 issue featured Andrews's June 23 letter banning the *Labor News.*

Winnipeg Printing and Engraving Co. Ltd., Gentlemen: Certain members of the Winnipeg Western Labor News Special Strike edition have contained objectionable matter in that it is seditious, inflammatory and inciting to riot, and this publication must be discontinued. No more issues of this publication must be printed or circulated.

"Yours truly," ALFRED J. ANDREWS, "Agent, Department of Justice."

Dixon's comment followed.

Yesterday afternoon the letter provided at the head of this article was received by the Winnipeg Printing and Engraving Company. It came like a bolt from the blue. No warning of any kind had been given. The Labor News had been issued as a daily since the strike commenced. It has been circulated freely throughout Winnipeg and widely distributed throughout Canada. It has endeavoured to tell the truth, the whole truth and nothing but the truth. One would have thought that if it contained objectionable matter that the authorities would at least have issued some warning instead of summarily suppressing the paper as they have done. British fair play would have guaranteed some notice, some warning. But British fair play is a thing of the past in Winnipeg…This looks like a deliberate infringement of freedom of the press…But as fast as the authorities close one channel of truth another will open…The miserable tactics of the opposition simply serves to stiffen the determination of the strikers to win.

The next day, Dixon again changed the name of the strikers' paper— this time to the *Enlightener.*[26] It featured the editorial "Who's the Anarchist" and a notice about the strike's end. "General Sympathetic Strike Called Off for Thursday at 11:00 A.M.," read the announcement, accompanied by "Conditions: 'The Provincial Government have [*sic*] appointed a Commission to make a thorough investigation regarding re-instatement of all workers.'"

THE ENLIGHTENER

Published by The Press Committee

Winnipeg, Manitoba, Wednesday, June 25th, 1919 — No. 1

General Sympathetic

STRIKE CALLED OFF

For Thursday At 11 a.m.

CONDITIONS: The Provincial Government have appointed a Commission to make a thorough investigation regarding re=instatement of all Workers.

The *Enlightener*, June 25.

In a letter to his wife after the strike, Woodsworth described how authorities unsuccessfully tried to stop the printing of Dixon's June 25 *Enlightener*.[27]

> *So the next day* [June 25] *the labor boys worked the starting of a new paper without permission...They hadn't enough type, so they "borrowed" some from another newspaper office in the same building. Those interested in stopping the paper got out a warrant to hold the type, but it seems they couldn't, on a technicality, stop the press. So, with a bailiff and three special police looking on helplessly, the new paper was run off! All this time Dixon was in hiding, writing clandestinely for dear life.*

Also on June 25, the *Ottawa Journal* ran one of John Conklin's final dispatches. In "End of Winnipeg Strike After Weeks of Distress and Big Loss to Everybody," he updated events. "Some of the firemen, postal workers and policemen have lost out for good. That fact seems inevitable. That is where the city of Winnipeg gains for the time being, if a Labor Council is not in control next year, which is among the possibilities."

The next day, in "Finish of 'Peg Strike Finds Many Men Out," Plewman offered several reasons for the strike's failure.

> *Opponents of sympathetic strikes say that none ever has been a success. The one in Winnipeg, they say, might have been an exception to the rule had the leaders not pulled out the workers who supplied food and operated public utilities and postal services. That, with the fear of Bolshevism, aroused community spirit in Winnipeg as it never before had been aroused and thousands of business men neglected their businesses and homes, sacrificed large sums of money and served as ordinary laborers in order to break the strike. Winnipeg's community spirit undoubtedly was the deciding factor in the struggle, with the power of the Provincial and Federal Government as the next most important feature.*

Plewman's final dispatch appeared in the *Star* the day after the strike ended. In "Andrews the Brains of Strike Opponents," Plewman adroitly identified the Citizens executive member as the individual most responsible for defeating the strike.[28] Plewman began his account by comparing Andrews to strike leader Bob Russell.

> *If R.B. Russell, the Socialist machinist was the outstanding leader of the Winnipeg general strike, A.J. Andrews. K.C., was the principal human*

factor in opposing the strike movement. Those two men were generals directing the strategy of opposing forces. Unlike in age, appearance, training and ideals, they were not unequal rivals. Andrews himself would be the first to admit that Russell is well-posted as to economics and labor organization and a man of rather more than ordinary native ability. The battle between these two clever tacticians provided a fascinating study apart from the magnitude of the national issue involved. Russell was not worsted until Andrews was given the opportunity to use the powers of the State to put Russell in custody and eliminate him as a factor in the strike. Andrews is old enough to be Russell's father. His hair, long in front and rather thin, is iron grey and often tousled. His face is clean shaven, with a pipe usually in the mouth. He is not at all finicky about his clothes and general appearance. Andrews often was seen during the strike, hatless, with a wilted collar dashing about the city.

Then Plewman focused solely on Andrews.

He was here, there and everywhere, directing the operations of the Citizens' Committee of One Thousand, as a member of the executive, finding and assembling evidence against the strike leaders, as a representative of the Department of Justice drawing up charges, directing raids, supervising arrests and holding innumerable conferences with the authorities, business and labor leaders. It is an open secret that the Citizens' Committee dictated nearly every move made during the strike by the Council. Council readily followed intimations that the police force should be dismissed, pledges against sympathetic strikes be exacted from all civic employees, various police utilities be operated by volunteers, a monster force of special police be recruited at six dollars a day, and ice and milk be distributed from the schools. Probably no one person had more to do with these various moves than had Mr. Andrews. He is credited with having had a hand in framing the change in the Immigration Act rushed through Parliament in one hour, which would permit British-born agitators to be deported after summary trial, and he certainly was responsible for the sensational round-up of the strike leaders and their imprisonment in a penitentiary twenty miles from the city. Enlistment of a large citizen army, use of the North-west Mounted Police, forcing the railway company to operate the street cars, are all moves supposed to have been made after Andrews had voiced his approval.

Before the strike officially ended at 11:00 a.m. on June 26, both Dixon and Dafoe provided commentaries.[29] In "What Next? Lessons for All," Dixon summarized what labor had learned from the strike and what would be its next goal.

> The next fight will be in the political field. Unless the Union Government[30] is driven in the country, the next municipal election will be the scene of action. There must be no 9-5, 9-5, 9-5 upon city council.[31] Labor constitutes a majority of the citizens and it should have a majority representation upon city council…Labor was not prepared for the long and bitter struggle which was forced upon her by the bosses six weeks ago. But in spite of her unpreparedness labor made a magnificent fight. Now get ready for the next fight….Never say die. Carry on.

Dafoe used "The Collapse" to explain who had instigated the strike and why it had failed.

> It was a strike deliberately engineered by Reds and planned long in advance; it was a "tryout" in Canada of the methods which had been given their first test in Seattle…The Reds who planned the strike…saw certain advantages in selecting Winnipeg as the point at which the revolution was to start… The plans of the Reds were well laid and most of their calculations were justified by the event…The miscalculation which proved fatal to their scheme was their entire failure to realize the effect of their wanton attacks upon the people, upon public opinion…In essence this was a victory for the plain people who rose in wrath against the pretensions of the strike committee.

On June 28, Magee wrote the *Telegram*'s final strike editorial, "Let Us Reason Together."

> There ought to be no spirit of exultation manifest or felt on the part of those who were instrumental in defeating the attacks made upon our democracy and our British institutions by some thousands of our citizens who were misled by a handful of revolutionaries and anarchists. The loyal citizens of Winnipeg have won a hard-fought fight. They naturally feel gratified with their victory—but the manly victor never kicks the body of his fallen foe, nor cheers his own triumph.

Magee then argued for conciliation by employers.

> *It has come to the attention of The Telegram that some employers have refused to employ any person who has been on strike without a grievance. This might be a natural position for one to adopt in a moment of extreme irritation. But it is not the position that big men will adopt after calm reflection. The business of the city must be re-established. It must proceed.*

However, there were limits to Magee's generosity.

> *This charity that The Telegram earnestly advocates ought not to be applied to those who deliberately and knowingly precipitated our catastrophe. They deserve deeper punishment than they have brought down upon themselves—a deeper punishment, even, than they are likely to suffer. They should be permanently black-listed. They should be made to wander abroad. It should be a standing rule of all employers that no agitator, known as such, should find work in the city.*

EPILOGUE

Two years after the strike was defeated, *Free Press* editor John Dafoe still connected it to Lenin and the Russian Revolution by insisting that it "was a made-to-order strike for revolutionary or semi-revolutionary purposes by Reds…Some really thought it would start something that would bring about actual Revolution as in Russia."[32] Was the strike as claimed by Dafoe and the Citizens caused by Reds/Bolshevists intent on revolution, or was it, as the Strike Committee insisted, really about legitimate labour demands of wages, work conditions and union recognition? This question remained unanswered until 1949, when historian Donald Masters investigated the event's causes and effects and the next year published *The Winnipeg General Strike*. The weight of evidence led him to conclude that Bolshevists had not engineered the strike, nor had the One Big Union directed it. While it is fair to say that subsequent historians and strike scholars have not always agreed on the event's causes, interpretation and significance, most have concurred with Masters that it was not a revolutionary plot.

The strike lasted forty-two days. Yet, beyond longevity, what did it achieve? There were virtually no gains for trade unionists; in fact, 119 telephone workers, 403 postal employees and 53 firemen lost their former jobs. The June 21 riot of Bloody Saturday near City Hall resulted in 2 dead, dozens hospitalized and scores of citizens arrested. Finally, following the dispute, the private prosecution of several strike leaders directed by leading Citizens member Alfred Andrews sent 6 strike leaders to prison and left a decades-long legacy of bitterness among the city's working class.

As one local labour organizer astutely observed, "There was never in history a strike in which the workers answered the call so spontaneously, and there never was a strike in which the workers were so badly trimmed."

Despite being "trimmed," the strikers did experience two positive outcomes, with the first coming sooner than expected. Following the strike, a provincial investigation into its causes and events was undertaken by Manitoba judge H.A. Robson. His enquiry took place in Winnipeg during open sessions between July 10 and September 16, 1919. After eleven days of hearings, he determined that the strike was based in a protest against difficult postwar living conditions, including the high cost of living, inadequate wages and profiteering.

The second outcome was the emergence of labour as a political force. Arrested but not convicted strike leaders Abraham Heaps and James Woodsworth became longtime members of Parliament and helped establish the Co-Operative Commonwealth Federation Party. Jailed strike leaders William Ivens and George Armstrong, along with acquitted Labour MLA Fred Dixon, attained success in provincial politics, and imprisoned John Queen eventually served as mayor of Winnipeg seven times during the Depression. Bob Russell, who was given the longest sentence of two years in the strike trials, came close to electoral success at both the provincial and federal levels and championed the One Big Union in Winnipeg for thirty years.

NOTES

Setting the Scene

1. Johnson used the byline "Main Johnson" because his mother's maiden name was Main.

Chapter 1

2. In addition to the *Vancouver Daily Province*, Porter provided strike dispatches for the *Vancouver Daily Sun*, *Edmonton Bulletin*, *Calgary Herald*, *Toronto Evening Telegram* and *Montreal Star*.
3. During the preliminary hearing of the strike leaders in August 1919, testimony revealed that Travers Sweatman and Fletcher Sparling were the *Winnipeg Citizen*'s editors. Public Archives of Manitoba, M 268 Preliminary Hearing, *The King v. William Ivens, R.J. Johns et al.*, testimony of Frederick Thompson, 5 August 1919. Charles Roland has also been identified as a strong possibility for the position in Kramer and Mitchell, *When the State Trembled*, 347. The author has amalgamated Sweatman, Sparling and Roland into the "editor."

4. Adams's story was published in *Collier's* on July 19, 1919.

5. On May 18, Johnson interviewed Ivens in the Labor Temple and was told that the paper's editor was censoring strike news leaving Winnipeg. As a result of this interview, Johnson was subpoenaed by the Crown to testify on August 1, 1919, at Ivens's preliminary hearing on charges of seditious conspiracy.

6. "Opera bouffe" was a genre of late nineteenth-century French operetta known for elements of comedy, satire, parody and farce.

7. In addition to the *Toronto Star*, Conklin provided strike dispatches for the *Halifax Chronicle*, *Halifax Herald*, *Montreal Star*, *Ottawa Journal*, *Hamilton Spectator*, *London Advertiser*, *London Free Press*, *Vancouver Daily Sun* and *Vancouver Daily Province*.

8. Ivens was born in England.

9. Bob Russell, Harry Veitch, Ernie Robinson and James Winning were members of the Strike Committee, and Ivens was editor of the *Western Labor News*.

CHAPTER 2

10. When the WTLC called the strike, the executive asked each of the one hundred unions involved in the walkout to appoint two delegates to a Strike Committee. Later, this was increased to three delegates, giving the General Strike Committee three hundred members. The WTLC then elected by ballot five members, in addition to the executive officers, to be the nucleus of the Strike Committee. From this Strike Committee, a Central Strike Committee of fifteen was later struck. The General Strike Committee decided all matters of policy and appointed all subsidiary committees, such as press, relief, organization and food.

11. In breaking with agency practice, Livesay signed the dispatch.

12. The Citizens ads in the *Tribune* and *Free Press* (such as "Bolshevism—or Fruitful Order," "The Alien in Our Midst," "Red Flag or Union Jack" and "Canadians or Revolutionist…Which?") were similar to those in the *Telegram*.

13. In his dispatches to the *Toronto Telegram*, correspondent Garnet Porter consistently supported the Citizens, and it is probable that he influenced Snider to do the same in her reporting.

14. A reference to Ivens's "Do Nothing" advice to strikers.

15. During his strike coverage, Evans also acted as a "special correspondent" for the *Port Arthur Daily News-Chronicle*.

CHAPTER 3

16. *Leslie's* published Hare's photo-story on June 21, 1919.
17. A reference to the number of strikers and the Citizens' Committee of One Thousand.
18. George W. Allan was elected a Unionist member to the House of Commons in the December 1917 election. During the strike, he served as a liaison for the Citizens to the federal government.

CHAPTER 4

19. Woodsworth acted as editor and Dixon as reporter/editor.

CHAPTER 5

20. The exact number of militia used on June 21 is not known, but by then, Ketchen had a total force of 326 officers and 4,295 enlisted men.
21. Among the papers that carried Livesay's June 23 exclusive were the *Calgary Morning Albertan, Regina Morning Leader, Toronto World, Ottawa Citizen* and *Montreal Herald.*
22. It is not certain *when* Gray read the Riot Act. From contemporary newspaper accounts, it was just as likely that the mounted RNWMP fired into the crowd *before* or *during* rather than *after* Gray read the act. If the shot that killed bystander Mike Sokolowski was fired *before* the Riot Act was read, the killing might be construed as murder by an unsympathetic jury. However, if the Riot Act was read first, that was notice to all that military had replaced civil control and a state of war existed for the time being between the authorities and the crowd.
23. Controversy remains concerning the death of Sokolowski. In his June 21 dispatch, Livesay reported that Sokolowski was killed "while crossing the street," but two days later, the *Free Press* claimed that he was killed "presumably while stooping to pick up a missile." Fred Dixon reported in the *Enlightener* that Sokolowski was simply an innocent bystander who was shot accidentally.
24. Livesay, *Making of a Canadian*, 82–83.

CHAPTER 6

25. After Andrews banned the paper, Dixon was forced to change the name of the *Western Labor News*.
26. Another name change was required after Andrews banned the *Western Star*.
27. Cited in McNaught, *Prophet in Politics*, 128.
28. Plewman's identification of Andrews as the individual most responsible for defeating the strike has been conclusively established by Kramer and Mitchell. According to veteran Canadian journalist and Dafoe biographer George Ferguson, the strike coverage by Plewman and fellow reporter Main Johnson was one of the factors in the *Star* eventually winning the circulation battle with the rival evening paper *Toronto Telegram*. Library and Archives Canada, Michael Dupuis Collection, MG 31 B 10, Letter to Dupuis from George Ferguson, March 6, 1972.
29. Ivens resumed editorship of the *Labor News* on June 27 at 7:00 p.m. Minutes later, editor-in-hiding Dixon walked into to the Rupert Street police station and surrendered to a most surprised sergeant in charge.
30. The Union government had been elected in December 1917.
31. A reference to the five Labour members on the fourteen-member City Council.

EPILOGUE

32. Cited in Cook, *Politics of John W. Dafoe*, 101.

BIBLIOGRAPHY

ARCHIVES

Library and Archives Canada, Michael Dupuis Collection, MG 31 B 10.
Public Archives of Manitoba, M 268 Preliminary Hearing. *The King v. William Ivens, R.J. Johns et al.*

BOOKS AND ARTICLES

Adams, Samuel Hopkins. "The One Big Union." *Collier's* (July 19, 1919).
Bercuson, David. *Confrontation in Winnipeg: Labour, Industrial Relations and the General Strike*. Montreal: McGill-Queen's University Press, 1994.
Bumsted, J.M. *The Winnipeg General Strike of 1919: An Illustrated History*. Winnipeg: Watson Dwyer Publishing, 1994.
Cook, Ramsay. *The Politics of John W. Dafoe and the Free Press*. Toronto: University of Toronto Press, 1963.
Dupuis, Michael. "Manitoba's Own Kentucky Colonel." *Manitoba History* 60 (February 2009).

———. "Remembering John J. Conklin." *Manitoba History* 54 (February 2007).

———. "The *Toronto Star* and the Winnipeg General Strike." *Manitoba History* 49 (June 2005).

Earl, Marjorie, ed. *Torch on the Prairies: A Portrait of Journalism in Manitoba, 1859–1988*. Winnipeg: Winnipeg Press Club, 1999.

Friedheim, Robert. *The Seattle General Strike*. Seattle: University of Washington, 1964.

Hare, James H. "Canada's Fight Against Bolshevism." *Leslie's Weekly* (June 21, 1919).

Harkness, Ross. *J.E. Atkinson of the Star*. Toronto: University of Toronto Press, 1963.

Kramer, Reinhold, and Tom Mitchell. *When the State Trembled*: *How A.J. Andrews and the Citizens' Committee Broke the Winnipeg General Strike*. Toronto: University of Toronto Press, 2010.

Lang, Marjory. *Women Who Made the News: Female Journalists in Canada, 1880–1945*. Montreal: McGill-Queen's University Press, 1999.

Livesay, J.F.B. *The Making of a Canadian*. Toronto: Ryerson Press, 1947.

Masters, D.C. *The Winnipeg General Strike*. Toronto: University of Toronto Press, 1950.

McNaught, Kenneth. *A Prophet in Politics: A Biography of J.S. Woodsworth*. Toronto: University of Toronto Press, 1959.

Penner, Norman, ed. *Winnipeg 1919*: *The Strikers' Own History of the Winnipeg General Strike*. Toronto: James Lewis and Samuel, 1973.

Poulton, Ron. *The Paper Tyrant: John Ross Robertson of the Toronto Telegram*. Toronto: Clarke, Irwin & Company, 1971.

DOCUMENT COLLECTIONS

Conklin, Robert. *Family History of the Conklins in Canada*. Richmond, British Columbia: self-published, n.d. Private Collection.

Johnson, Main. Special File. Toronto: Toronto Daily Star Library, 1972.

Plewman, William. Special File. Toronto: Toronto Daily Star, 1972.

Newspapers

Chicago Tribune.
Enlightener.
Halifax Chronicle.
Halifax Herald.
Hamilton Spectator.
Manitoba Free Press.
Montreal Star.
Ottawa Journal.
Toronto Daily Star.
Toronto Evening Telegram.
Toronto Star Weekly.
Vancouver Daily Province.
Vancouver Sun.
Western Labor News.
Western Star.
Winnipeg Citizen.
Winnipeg Telegram.
Winnipeg Tribune.

Pamphlets/Booklets

Berkowski, Gerry, and Nolan Reilly. *1919: The Winnipeg General Strike, a Driving and Walking Tour.* Winnipeg: Manitoba Culture, Heritage and Recreation, 1986.

Komus, Matthew. *Winnipeg's Exchange District.* Winnipeg: Exchange District BIZ, 2006.

INDEX

ABOUT THE AUTHOR

Michael Dupuis is a retired Canadian history teacher and writer. Since 2005, he has published work in several academic journals, commercial magazines and newspapers in Canada, the United States and the United Kingdom. His writing concentrates on the role played by journalists in historical events, including the Winnipeg General Strike, the *Titanic* disaster, the Halifax Explosion, the On to Ottawa Trek and the Regina Riot. In 2011, he was a consultant for Danny Schur's Winnipeg General Strike documentary *Mike's Bloody Saturday* and an advisor to the Canadian Broadcasting Corporation for the television special *Titanic: The Canadian Story*. In 2012, he contributed the chapter "Canadian Journalists in New York" in *Titanic Century: Media, Myth, and the Making of a Cultural Icon*. He holds a BA (English) and MA (history) from the University of Ottawa and a BEd from the University of Toronto. Michael resides in Victoria, British Columbia, with his wife, Christine Moore, and their two golden retrievers.